SHARED VOICES

HEIDI RAINES

SHARED VOICES

A Framework for Patient and Employee
Safety in Healthcare

Forbes | Books

Published by Forbes Books, Charleston, South Carolina.
Member of Advantage Media.

Forbes Books is a registered trademark, and the Forbes Books colophon is a trademark of Forbes Media, LLC.

Printed in the United States of America.

10 9 8 7 6 5 4 3 2 1

ISBN: 979-8-88750-094-2 (Paperback)
ISBN: 979-8-88750-095-9 (eBook)

LCCN: 2022919637

Cover design by Danna Steele
Layout design by Matthew Morse
Graphic design by Douglas Miller

This custom publication is intended to provide accurate information and the opinions of the author in regard to the subject matter covered. It is sold with the understanding that the publisher, Forbes Books, is not engaged in rendering legal, financial, or professional services of any kind. If legal advice or other expert assistance is required, the reader is advised to seek the services of a competent professional.

Since 1917, Forbes has remained steadfast in its mission to serve as the defining voice of entrepreneurial capitalism. Forbes Books, launched in 2016 through a partnership with Advantage Media, furthers that aim by helping business and thought leaders bring their stories, passion, and knowledge to the forefront in custom books. Opinions expressed by Forbes Books authors are their own. To be considered for publication, please visit **books.Forbes.com**.

To Danny, Marie, Cecilia, and Camille
You are the greatest gifts I've ever received
Your love leads me to great adventures

• • •

To healthcare workers, leaders, and patients
Your voices are the first step in meaningful transformation

CONTENTS

PART III

Introduction

Midlevel healthcare providers, registered nurses, medical assistants, and technicians deliver approximately 88 percent of all healthcare in the United States at over two and a half million points of care.[1] That latter number is growing, as people turn to retail health centers, pharmacies, and telemedicine for basic healthcare services as well as vaccinations. An increasing number of points of care is potentially a very good development insofar as it suggests increased—and timelier—patient access to needed services. However, as points of care continue to grow in number, there is a corresponding need to put in place structures designed to support better, safer, and more equitable care. As points of care grow and training levels vary, it is paramount for healthcare leaders to establish a framework that sets caregivers up for success at every level and in every type of healthcare organization. My primary goal—in my work, in my advocacy, and in this book—is to equip these organizations with a framework of how near-miss and incident reporting, equitable follow-up, analysis, and learning are all

---

1   "Registered Nurses Made Up 30 Percent of Hospital Employment in May 2019," TED: The Economics Daily, US Bureau of Labor Statistics, updated April 27, 2020, https://www.bls.gov/opub/ted/2020/ registered-nurses-made-up-30-percent-of-hospital-employment-in-may-2019.htm.

essential parts of achieving a just culture of care and of protecting patients, safeguarding and giving voice to employees, and elevating the overall health of our communities.

My second—and closely related—goal is to inform policy makers and other high-level decision makers of the specific benefits of transforming healthcare organizations into safe cultures of care. Ensuring patient safety, increasing and sustaining quality of care, and supporting employee safety all require that resources be dedicated to modernizing patient safety and incident reporting technology in all points of care.

· · ·

I've always had a predisposition for what's called "systems thinking." This approach to problem-solving involves taking a broad view of structures and patterns to understand the ways individual parts fit together as a whole. As a child, I found patterns everywhere. It felt natural to connect the dots between cause and effect; line that up with dates, times, and places; and then logically sort behaviors and events to create a sense of order and safety. This allowed me to manage and endure the health-related issues I witnessed and even experienced firsthand at a very young age.

I grew up in a rural southern town with limited access to healthcare. My parents were self-employed, and healthcare—let alone health insurance—was a luxury that they were not consistently able to provide. We received required care—immunizations and the like—from community and state-run clinics but otherwise only sought out medical assistance when faced with an emergency. This lack of access to needed care as a child led to hearing loss that remains with me today and shaped my passion for equitable access to quality care for all, especially those who, like I did, belong to underserved groups.

There were few women leaders in our town; one was the physician at our local primary care clinic. She served her patients and our community well, providing quality care and offering a sliding scale for payment when health insurance was not an option. Looking back, I now realize she was the first servant leader I encountered. As her teenage patient, I felt drawn to her as a role model, and once I came of age to work—and understood that employment at the clinic would give me access to needed care—I asked her for a job. From my seat at the front desk, I heard patients' concerns and perspectives and observed the daily tasks of the clinical staff. Over time, I developed a better understanding of the challenges surrounding access to care, issues of care quality, and the unwavering commitment of most frontline clinical care staff to provide the best care possible within the constraints of organizational systems and with the resources available to them.

From working as a teenager at a rural health clinic to my positions today—founder of the healthcare technology company Performance Health Partners (PHP), co-owner of an ambulatory surgery center, and patient and healthcare worker advocate—my career has revolved around understanding and supporting the well-being of healthcare organizations, healthcare workers, and patients. I have advocated for and designed solutions to ensure that, no matter the size of the patient population, healthcare organizations have access to the knowledge and technology tools they need to deliver safe, equitable, and quality care. I've made it my professional life's work to identify the roles that systems and processes play in creating safety incidents and to find solutions that improve the environment of care and support overall patient and employee well-being.

Since those early days, I have had the privilege of working to create systemic change within healthcare organizations, from rural community clinics to national health systems, and for specialized care models like telehealth, behavioral health, and social services. I have worked with one of the most innovative technology companies in the world to build incident reporting and employee health solutions that promote safe and equitable care for their employees. What all these healthcare organizations have in common is that they embrace event reporting as a pathway to preventing harm—to achieving greater patient and employee safety and a higher quality of care for the communities they serve. Performance Health Partners' software was developed from our team's experiences working within a variety of healthcare organizations and is rooted in the belief that organizations of all sizes should have access to technology solutions that are financially obtainable and immediately and easily functional within their care settings. Furthermore, the software was designed to empower employees to proactively monitor their workplaces and participate in efforts that directly affect their environments of care for the better.

The following chapters share how organizations have transformed from viewing incident reporting as a negative occurrence to seeing incident reporting as a means of prevention. We will see that it *is* possible to incorporate incident reporting tools and quality-rounding checklists in a way that gives voice to patients and to employees who are the eyes, ears, and heartbeat of a healthcare organization.

A measurable improvement in the quality and cost of care in the US health system *can* be achieved by providing structural and financial resources for modernizing patient safety technology. The quality of a healthcare system is only as good as the quality of care at each single point of care. When we discuss increasing the quality of care in the United States, we must look at *all* points of care and ask: Do they have access to the technology tools and resources needed to deliver the same quality of care, regardless of the socioeconomic status of the community they serve?

* * *

The perspectives offered throughout this book reflect the many lenses through which I have viewed our healthcare system. As a patient without insurance or access to needed care. As a hospital administrator who's witnessed firsthand how leadership and organizational culture can influence safety and the quality of care. As a preceptor faculty member in Tulane's Master of Healthcare Administration program, where I've been training the next generations of healthcare leaders for over a decade. And as a social entrepreneur in health tech, a role in which I, along with a stellar team of talented individuals, develop and implement solutions to culture-based and systems-driven challenges in healthcare.

This array of experiences has helped me understand that some organizations are more receptive than others to focusing on learning and innovation. Those who have committed to transforming into a just safety culture have instilled in me a sense of possibility, earnest optimism, and confidence in people's abilities to voice observations to drive positive change.

* * *

In the coming years, how can we, as healthcare organizations, care-givers, and leaders work toward creating a nonpunitive, inclusive, more just culture delivering high-quality care? The pages that follow offer practical steps that healthcare organizations—no matter their size, location, or available resources—can use to work toward better communication, increased modernization, and a renewed focus on employee safety. We'll look at how providers can implement technology frameworks that identify and respond to incidents, and we'll map out plans for transitioning from a retroactive to a proactive system of accountability. I'll share stories in which the use of data collection and pattern finding drive intentional improvement and support the staff at the very heart of our healthcare system—the people who deliver hands-on care to patients.

It is from and within people's stories that innovation and transformation occur. Suppose we can find a way to hear what employees, patients, and patient families have to say and to process that information for the sole purpose of pursuing positive change. In that case, we can get closer than ever before to achieving an environment of zero harm. When we're all caught up in the same old stories, our systems will achieve the same old results. But if we muster the courage to ask some very basic questions, keep asking them until they're answered, and listen without judgment to those answers, we'll uncover modifications, small and large, that can lead to impactful change.

PART I

CHAPTER 1

Just Culture in Healthcare

[T]he single greatest impediment to error prevention
is that we punish people for making them.

—Dr. Lucian Leape, professor, Harvard School of Public Health,
testimony before Congress on healthcare quality improvement[2]

I t was a particularly grueling night in the high-volume urban ER where Nadia was the physician supervisor. Midway through the shift, two of Nadia's patients were discharged at the same time. One of them was a teenager with bronchitis, and the other was a little girl with asthma. While running among multiple patients, Nadia mistakenly entered discharge paperwork for the teenager instead of the girl. The charge nurse who had cared for both patients along with Nadia was on her lunch break, so it was an alternate nurse who completed the discharge process and gave the mom of the girl the teenager's paperwork.

---

2   VHA's Risk Management Policy and Performance: Hearing before the Subcommittee on Health of the Committee on Veterans' Affairs, Serial No. 105-23, October 8, 1997, https://www.govinfo.gov/content/pkg/CHRG-105hhrg46316/pdf/CHRG-105hhrg46316.pdf.

Not minutes thereafter, Nadia recognized her error. She telephoned the mother of the girl to explain what had happened and determine how to get the correct paperwork to the right person. Mother and child returned to the ER within minutes, and all was resolved. Next, Nadia stepped over to the computer and formally submitted an incident report in which she acknowledged giving the discharge papers to the incorrect patient and described how she had resolved the error.

This was Nadia's first year in a new position, and at her next performance review, her manager focused the entire review on this single discharge error. Nadia felt the need to ask: "Am I on probation or getting fired?" Her manager's reply was that the two of them just needed to acknowledge that they addressed the matter.

That a quickly resolved paperwork error became the focus for assessing Nadia's overall performance ended up having a profound effect on her attitude: "That was the end of reporting for me. I've yet to fill out another report. I'm pretty meticulous on my rotations, but I do make mistakes. I see other people make mistakes too. But if what I experienced is how mistakes are dealt with, then I'm clearly not part of improving this culture or the larger organization that we work within. So now I just come to work and go home, and I try to fly under the radar."

In Nadia's organization, senior leaders were interested in assigning blame to an individual for a reported error rather than learning from the event and implementing system process improvements or training reinforcements to prevent future incidents from occurring. In a culture like the one Nadia works in, employees tend to be motivated by fear and anxiety. They won't choose to speak out about patient safety issues because when they do, blame takes the place of acknowledgment, education, and an overall dedication to helping others avoid similar events. When a healthcare culture encourages silence and facilitates anxiety, it cuts down on employees' sense of possibility and creates fragility within the system overall.

Care Volume and Complexity in the Absence of Effective Systemization

The complexity and volume of healthcare delivery has increased, and the number of points of care and reliance on frontline care workers has grown tremendously. The United States is expected to see a shortage of up to nearly 122,000 physicians by 2032.[3] Healthcare organizations are increasingly turning toward the skill sets of entry-level-to-mid-level healthcare workers to help fill this service gap. According to the US Bureau of Labor Statistic's Occupational Outlook, occupational demand and job growth for entry level and midlevel healthcare staff is expected to grow three times faster than average in the ten-year period from 2020 to 2030. The numbers of medical assistants, technicians, home health aides, and personal care aides are growing the fastest; all play an essential role in care teams, and all spend their time directly interacting with patients. Home health aides and personal care aids are projected to grow 35 percent faster than any other occupations in the country, and medical assistant jobs are projected to grow 20 percent faster than other professions. Positions with more specific training, like nurse anesthetists and nurse practitioners, are projected to grow by 45 percent.[4]

---

3   "New Findings Confirm Predictions on Physician Shortage," Association of American Medical Colleges, updated April 23, 2019, https://www.aamc.org/news-insights/press-releases/new-findings-confirm-predictions-physician-shortage.

4   "Healthcare Occupations: Occupational Outlook Handbook," U.S. Bureau of Labor Statistics (U.S. Bureau of Labor Statistics, April 18, 2022), https://www.bls.gov/ooh/healthcare/home.htm.

People in healthcare work long, hard hours. They are struggling, however, to provide increasingly complex care in the absence of effective systemization. As the number of healthcare employees and points of care increase, the question of how best to support these workers to deliver high-quality care becomes ever more pressing. Healthcare professionals of all kinds should be asking: What is the framework or the infrastructure—the processes and checklists, for example—that will set our healthcare workers, patients, and patient caregivers up for success?

> Recognizing and implementing actions to prevent patient and employee harm has the greatest potential effect on the quality of care delivered in our healthcare systems, just as preventive care and wellness efforts slow or stop the progression of disease.

At the very least, we must modernize the systems that guide their work and enable their voices to be heard—especially when they see opportunities to prevent harm and improve care environments.

Many of us in healthcare entered the profession because we wanted to help, heal, and serve. At our cores, we have compassion, empathy, and a drive to enable people to live their best lives. That's a belief I hold onto after many years of managing healthcare organizations and working alongside them. Recognizing and implementing actions to prevent patient and employee harm has the greatest potential effect on the quality of care delivered in our healthcare systems, just as preventive care and wellness efforts slow or stop the progression of disease.

What Is a Just Culture in Healthcare?

The term *just culture* was first used in healthcare in a 2001 report by David Marx, which popularized the term in the patient safety lexicon.[5] *Just culture* refers to a system of shared accountability in which organizations are responsible for the systems they design and for responding to the behaviors of their employees in a fair and just manner. Employees are accountable for the quality of their choices and for reporting incidents and system vulnerabilities.[6] In a just culture, safety incidents are seen as *opportunities* to share observations about system risks and organizational behaviors.

A just culture is one in which people recognize both that competent professionals make mistakes and that the discovery of multiple or repeated incidents indicates solvable issues that arise between humans and the systems in which they work. A just culture accounts for *all factors* contributing to an incident, from the human to the environmental, technical, and so on.

In testimony before congress, Lucian Leape, MD, member of the Quality of Health Care in America Committee at the Institute of Medicine and faculty at the Harvard School of Public Health, noted that approaches that focus on punishing individuals instead of changing systems provide strong incentives for people to report only those errors they cannot hide: "Rather than reduce errors, punishment

---

5   Congress on Nursing Practice and Economics, ANA Position Statement: Just Culture, 2010.

6   "What Is Just Culture? Changing the Way We Think about Errors to Improve Patient Safety and Staff Satisfaction," Mass General Brigham, accessed August 23, 2022, https://www.brighamandwo-mensfaulkner.org/about-bwfh/news/what-is-just-culture-changing-the-way-we-think-about-errors-to-improve-patient-safety-and-staff-satisfaction.

increases them because it makes it difficult to uncover the underlying causes of errors and remedy them."[7]

To the contrary of a punitive system, a just culture creates and sustains an atmosphere of trust in which healthcare workers are supported and treated fairly when safety incidents occur in patient care. It creates an environment in which healthcare workers and patients feel safe to share observations and report concerns. Reports are acknowledged by all to be important sources of information about weaknesses in the system that need to be understood and addressed to improve patient safety. In addition to encouraging reporting, just cultures also utilize data to identify patterns; they begin with the assumption that many individual incidents represent predictable interactions between humans and the systems in which they work.

Key components of just culture include the following:

- Adopting one model of shared accountability and shared goals versus relying on multiple individual perceptions and attitudes toward goals and accountability
- Learning from events versus blaming individuals
- Distinguishing among and managing behavioral choices including human error, at-risk behavior, and reckless behavior versus assuming the worst in every instance
- Recognizing that incidents represent predictable interactions and provide opportunities for learning and prevention versus assuming each incident is a system anomaly and pursuing no preventive measures
- Designing safety into all clinical systems and processes and continually monitoring for systemic breakdowns versus

---

7   The Committees on Appropriations, Health, Education, Labor, and Pensions, and Veterans' Affairs, Joint Hearings before the Subcommittee on Labor, Health and Human Services, and Education, and Related Agencies (report, 2001).

attending only to individual actions and declining to collect and analyze data[8]

If we want to achieve a more just, proactive, and equitable culture in our US healthcare system, a culture that truly places the health and safety of patients and employees at the forefront, then we must work together to shift our organizational cultures so that they encourage reporting, focus on learning from observations, identify and resolve systemic issues, and, to the greatest extent possible, prevent those issues from occurring at all.

Steps toward Achieving a Just Culture of Care

1. Make Reporting Routine

When I meet leaders in healthcare organizations, I often begin with one simple query to get a read on the overall culture: "Tell me about patient safety events in your organization." If an organization's leadership responds with, "We don't have any patient safety events," I immediately know there's an issue. What's actually being conveyed to me in that moment is something more like, "*We don't encourage reporting about patient safety events.*" The reality is that all healthcare organizations experience safety events, and every healthcare professional has witnessed or participated in one. As humans, none of us are immune to mistakes, and certainly no healthcare organization has a perfect record. If the assessment expressed by leadership is that there are no safety events, then that culture does not support transparency and learning.

A culture of safety is defined as "an integrated pattern of individual and organizational behavior, based upon shared beliefs and values,

---

8   Jennifer Allyn, "Just Culture: Balancing Accountability with Quality and Safety," rsna.org, February 18, 2019, https://www.rsna.org/news/2019/february/just-culture-background.

that continuously seeks to minimize patient harm that may result from the processes of care delivery."[9] An organization's safety culture should operate within a just culture, one that positively recognizes team members who report safety incidents, establishes clear parameters for equitable treatment of those who report and are involved in patient safety events, and is committed to evaluating all contributing factors to those events.

But safety incidents are not the only occurrences that matter within a just culture of care. What are referred to as near misses or "good catches" are equally important, as are observations about unsafe conditions. The World Health Organization defines a near miss as "an error that has the potential to cause an adverse event (patient harm) but fails to do so because of chance or because it is intercepted." Near misses occur up to one hundred times more frequently than incidents with harm, and given that the root causes of safety incidents and near misses are quite similar, paying careful attention to near misses is an important pathway to preventing future adverse events.

Proactive organizations reframe outdated attitudes around reporting to arrive at the shared belief that reporting is a tool for *understanding* processes, *learning* from near misses and safety incidents alike, and *pursuing improvements* in systems and procedures that yield measurable and ongoing improvements of the environment of care.

That mindset shift is as much about how executives, administrators, and managers think about patient safety events as it is about what happens among staff members who come into direct contact with any number of patients on a daily and hourly basis. Even if or when there are accessible reporting systems in place that could help facilitate a

9   P. Aspden, J. M. Corrigan, and J. Wolcott, et al., eds., Patient Safety: Achieving a New Standard of Care (Washington, DC: National Academies Press, 2004), https://www.ncbi.nlm.nih.gov/books/NBK216084/.

more just culture, if leadership focuses only on human factors and does not dig into the broader systemic issues influencing the event, they ultimately contribute to sustaining a punitive environment in which team members remain disinclined to trust the very systems and people that govern their work.

One-third of all harmful incidents affecting patients are deemed preventable.[10] An estimated 161,250 preventable deaths occur each year in US healthcare organizations.[11] Preventable safety incidents are estimated to cost the US healthcare system approximately $187.5 billion to $250 billion annually. When healthcare organizations make a concerted effort to shift from an incident-punishing and incident-hiding culture to a reporting and learning culture, those organizations focus more, and more deeply, on the safety of patients and healthcare professionals. The reason for this is clear: a commitment to safety is not a matter of mere rhetoric. When there is a culture firmly in place that supports employee and patient reporting—one that can appropriately analyze all factors that led up to a safety incident or near miss and that offers nonpunitive alternatives for following up on reported observations and events—an organization will identify the root causes of events sooner and save lives by doing so.

2. Give Employees, Patients, and Caregivers Voices

Establishing a just culture of care requires determination and persistence; it's no temporary fix or mere symptom alleviation. It begins

---

10   J. Wright et al., "Improving Patient Safety through the Involvement of Patients: Development and Evaluation of Novel Interventions to Engage Patients in Preventing Patient Safety Incidents and Protecting Them against Unintended Harm," Programme Grants for Applied Research 4, no. 15 (October 2016), https://pubmed.ncbi.nlm.nih.gov/27763744/.

11   Maria Castellucci, "161,000 Avoidable Deaths Occur in Hospitals Annually, Leapfrog Group Finds," Modern Healthcare, updated May 15, 2019, www.modernhealthcare.com/safety-quality/161000-avoidable-deaths-occur-hospitals-annually-leapfrog-group-finds.

with a clear-eyed and courageous look at the uncomfortable and imperfect parts of healthcare delivery and a commitment to pursuing organizational evolution by making systemic change without passing judgment and unfairly assigning blame. Organizations that commit to the reporting process push through initial and sometimes difficult discoveries, moving from acknowledgment, to awareness, to learning, and eventually, to prevention. It's only when we choose to access the extraordinary opportunity to give care providers, patients, and patient families voices—only when we speak up, learn, and adjust our practices intentionally and incrementally—that we make strides toward better care, lower costs, healthier employees, and safer patients.

Everyone involved in patient care should have an opportunity to voice their observations and provide feedback to remain vigilant against patient safety incidents. Healthcare teams must feel empowered to provide input when they think there could be more efficient ways of managing the environment of care. Just as much as employees need to be encouraged to report safety incidents and near misses, patients and their caregivers should be encouraged to provide information through an accessible reporting system.

The transition to a just culture is not only about our shift from punitive action to learning; it's also a transition in which organizational learning shifts from being focused primarily on problem-solving to being open to sharing information and stories, generating questions, and brainstorming solutions, all for the sake of improving the quality of care for the communities we serve. When healthcare workers and patients have voices without fear of retribution, it becomes possible to learn from incidents and near misses and to make changes that eventually shift an entire culture toward proactively seeking out opportunities to improve systems and processes.

3. Apply Systems Thinking

Early in my healthcare career, I had a penchant for systems thinking, but as a newcomer and the youngest administrator in the healthcare system in which I worked, I was also a person who felt "in over my head" with the level of responsibility that had been given me. My desire to learn about problems that arose and analyze how to solve those problems necessitated that I just keep asking questions—lots of questions. I tried to uncover the processes behind specific actions. Instead of asking questions like "Who did it?" I found myself asking, "How does this work? Why does it work this way?" or "Exactly where did the process break down?" Those were the very same questions that ultimately led me to develop solutions for improving systems, for supporting patient and employee safety, and for improving the environments in which care is delivered. Little did I know at the time that asking these questions is a key element of establishing a just culture. Much later in my career, I would learn that just cultures of care emphasize that incidents are generally the product of organizational cultures and systems rather than solely brought about by the person or persons directly involved. I would learn that in a just culture, after a patient safety incident, the question asked is "What went wrong?" rather than "Who caused the problem?" Systems thinking encourages questioning, a thorough understanding of linked causes, and problem-solving that provides safer and better patient-centered care.

According to the American Medical Association, systems thinkers embody fourteen habits. Systems thinkers and systems-thinking organizations

- seek to understand the big picture,
- observe how elements within a system change over time to generate patterns and trends,

- recognize that a system's structure generates behavior
- identify the circular nature of complex cause-and-effect relationships,
- make meaningful connections within and between systems,
- change perspectives to increase understanding,
- surface and test assumptions,
- consider the issue fully and resist coming to a quick conclusion,
- consider how mental models affect current reality and the future
- use understanding of system structure to identify possible actions
- consider short-term, long-term, and unintended consequences of actions
- recognize the impact of time delays when exploring cause-and-effect relationships, and
- check results and change actions if needed, a process known as "successive approximation."[12]

Focusing on entire systems rather than single individuals helps organizations get better at examining the complex causes of events and yields practical steps toward improving safety, efficiency, creativity, productivity, and even job satisfaction among employees. Often, it's incidents like Nadia's that occur—ones that avoid patient harm but nevertheless present opportunities to redesign systems, console the individuals involved, and if necessary, retrain teams.

---

12 Tanya Albert Henry, "Why You Need to Be a Systems Thinker in Health Care," American Medical Association, updated September 11, 2019, https://www.ama-assn.org/education/accelerating-change-medical-education/why-you-need-be-systems-thinker-health-care.

4. Modernize Systems

People have stories to tell about their experiences and their actions, and data, when thoroughly analyzed, has stories to tell as well. Data storytelling is an iterative exercise involving performing analysis from different angles, measuring, and comparing trends and associations to provide context and enlarge our understanding. Data offers us insights: through incident reporting and ongoing data collection, we can learn from multiple perspectives. The key is incorporating technologies that provide structure for recurring processes, help all parties have a voice, identify patterns and trends, and serve as a central repository for new learning and changed action.

One of the first organizations at which my team and I implemented a patient safety technology was a health system that was replacing its own home-grown incident reporting solution. The submission of events was quite effective with the homegrown solution, but there were clear issues with the follow-up process. We noticed, for example, that there were two risk managers keeping track of events on spreadsheets uploaded to a shared drive and that they were using email correspondence as a primary means of determining the details of reported events. We could also see that no matter how accurately they kept the data they'd collected for each independent event, it was nearly impossible to drill down into the details of specific events or to see any trends or correlations among the many events reported. They created a repository for data, but what they most needed was to analyze the data and place the information they collected into the hands of leaders and managers to remediate root causes—and to do so as quickly as possible.

By implementing a patient safety technology with activity management and data analytics, we were able to identify patterns that offered a more accurate story of what was occurring. One example still stands out to me from that early experience: the risk managers were aware of a high number of medication errors, but before we implemented real-time analytics, they did not have a way to quickly identify the root cause of those errors. A month after implementing our system, the organization learned that medication errors were occurring regularly in telemetry during the morning shift. They also learned that those errors did not result from the actions of the healthcare professionals on that floor during that shift. Instead, errors were occuring in the pharmacy, which was contracted out to a pharmacy management company. As a result of having access to this information, the organization was able to address recurring errors with the pharmacy contractor's systems and, in so doing, prevent future medication errors and improve patient safety and experience. Medication errors decreased. Patient experience improved. And caregiver morale improved because the medication reactions were identified as having a root cause firmly outside their control.

Impactful technology harnesses the power of many minds connecting academic research, best practices, and real-time human reporting and feedback to show us where we can do better and where we can get ahead by preventing future incidents from occurring. One mind may be capable of asking powerful questions, troubleshooting varieties of scenarios, and maximizing the potential to improve the environment of care. The best technologies support us by being intuitive to use and by harnessing the power of the many minds that make up an organization. Modernized technology provides a framework within which healthcare workers can ensure they're offering their best effort in the moment of care.

5. Emphasize Leadership's Influence

In a recent study that looked at trust among the nursing staff across a healthcare organization, trust in leaders was specifically defined as "the perception that clinical nurses will receive fair treatment from nurse leaders after an adverse event, regardless of their position in the hospital or the event's severity." A statistically significant finding of this research was that clinical nurses did not feel that their suggestions were respected or taken seriously by their supervisors, or that reported events were treated as opportunities for improvement. The authors concluded that this environment and ones like it were likely to be environments in which nurses may hesitate to report events or may develop behaviors that veer toward unnecessary risk-taking.[13]

The building blocks of trust are consistent, clear communication and the willingness to tackle difficult questions. Promoting a culture of safety is the responsibility of everyone within an organization—including leaders, frontline staff, contract personnel, and volunteers—but when it comes down to it, whether or not a just culture takes hold hinges on what executives and management do and the extent to which they actively cultivate the trust that is needed for reporting to become the norm rather than the exception. Given that achieving and sustaining trust is no easy task, the creation of a just culture requires daily commitment and consistent actions and reactions among leadership.

Along with leaders at all levels, executive leaders have significant roles to play in establishing and sustaining organizational culture precisely because they are the ones responsible for what happens after reporting. Consistency and predictability in the way an organization

---

13   Linda Paradiso and Nancy Sweeney, "Just Culture: It's More Than Policy," Nursing Management 50, no. 6 (June 2019): 38–45.

manages events contributes to establishing trust. It's most important that open and high-quality communication is practiced by leadership and that there is obvious and demonstrable commitment to continuous improvement. When the analysis of events is both careful and thorough, when there is meaningful training and education added in as needed, and when there is enthusiasm for information and knowledge sharing among teams, between departments, and with those in the highest leadership positions, fewer risks are likely to be taken, and both patients and the professionals who serve them are likely to experience better health outcomes.

When an organization is healthy, its leaders are not afraid of information. They know that they need accurate data to make decisions, and they encourage and emphasize the importance of reporting near misses. When healthcare professionals can see and address events that *almost happened*, they can take immediate action or address a situation before events *actually happen*. The payoff is that healthy organizations arrive at a point where the majority of, if not all, care teams are committed to the prevention of issues as they arise and before they become full-blown safety events.

"Oh, we intercepted a medication error this morning. Good catch! Now let's figure out how this happened to prevent it from occurring in the future." It's an extraordinary—but achievable—accomplishment when organizations don't simply accept reporting, learning, and sharing as norms but also celebrate them. Imagine acknowledging and celebrating the avoidance of a medication error, reporting that near miss, and after reporting, being able to trace back through related activities to determine how the incorrect medication was nearly dispensed. In a resilient organization with a just culture, placing emphasis fully on the side of patient and employee safety and prevention is a regular occurrence.

The Next Leap Forward

A just culture of care creates and sustains a mutually supportive and safe environment for patients and caregivers. I've witnessed firsthand organizations that embrace incident reporting and approach collected information as a means of building organizational trust, lessening anxiety and hypervigilance in their employees and patients, and evolving into an organization focused on prevention. In these organizations, healthcare staff know that they are not alone and that they are empowered to make choices that clearly contribute to preventing patient safety issues.

In healthcare professions, many of us pride ourselves on being part of cutting-edge and learning-progressive organizations. Sometimes that's true, but often, we're naming *goals* rather than realities. For that reason, I reemphasize here a point from earlier: the beginning of any organization's transformation toward becoming a just culture will likely be far from easy. At the frontiers of medicine are the leaders who dare to walk into uncharted territory, who are not afraid to fully acknowledge insights—whether directly from care providers or indirectly from data. It's only when we are forthcoming with observations, without the need to judge reported information as either good or bad, that we can begin to acknowledge elements of our organizations that need to be addressed to create a culture shift. It's only when we respect what others have to say about their observations and experiences that we can take that important leap toward establishing a just patient safety culture. If we don't back away from insight, we can begin to experience our potential as healthcare teams—all those accomplishments that we are capable of when we share knowledge with one another.

Modernizing patient safety and quality systems in our health-care organizations offers us the opportunity to make our stated goals realities. That shift—on which creating and sustaining a just culture relies—is our next great leap to equitable, safe, and quality care.

CHAPTER 2

Evolution of the Patient Safety Movement

The modern patient safety movement replaces "the blame and shame game" with an approach known as systems thinking. This paradigm acknowledges the human condition—namely, that humans err—and concludes that safety depends on creating systems that anticipate errors and either prevent or catch them before they cause harm. Such an approach has been the cornerstone of safety improvements in other high-risk industries but has been ignored in medicine until the past decade.

—Robert Wachter, MD, professor of medicine at University of California, San Francisco, *Understanding Patient Safety, Second Edition*

Emphasis on safety in healthcare has its roots as far back as nineteenth-century advocacy of washing one's hands before providing medical care. Health quality and safety did not categorically become policy issues in the United States until the late 1960s and not until academic research pointed out significant deficiencies within our healthcare systems. That research prompted initial efforts toward quality improvement, including instituting systems of reprimand

and reward, restructuring healthcare delivery and medical education, improving performance evaluation, and making those performance evaluations a matter of public record.

By the 1980s, efforts were geared toward heightening awareness of the need for improvements in patient safety and quality of care. By the early 1990s, researchers and healthcare practitioners were sharing information, creating educational opportunities, and collaborating on improvements. Then in the late 1990s, the US healthcare system witnessed the publication of two reports by President Clinton's Advisory Commission on Consumer Protection and Quality in the Health Care Industry. The *Consumer Bill of Rights and Responsibilities* appeared first, followed by *Quality First: Better Health Care for All Americans*.

It wasn't until the early 2000s that the industry focused its efforts on addressing patient safety and quality of care through tangible redesign of the US healthcare system. The shift toward redesign was motivated largely by media attention given to two more reports (these from the Institute of Medicine), one published in 1999 and titled *To Err Is Human: Building a Safer Health System* and another in 2001 titled *Crossing the Quality Chasm: A New Health System for the 21st Century*. Both reports helped accelerate healthcare redesign by pointing out challenges related to patient safety and healthcare quality and illuminated possibilities for improvement that required system-wide changes. With the help of all the public attention they received, the 1999 and 2001 reports galvanized concerted action when it came to preventing hospital deaths and injuries caused by medical errors.

Initial efforts made in response to these two reports focused on identifying and disciplining organizations and individuals who erred, *even though* the reports themselves were focused on strategies for incident *prevention*. Identifying patient safety events and holding practitioners accountable, while important steps toward increasing patient safety, are not all that is required to render entire healthcare systems safer. As the following graphic shows, the *To Err Is Human: Building Safer Health Systems* report included a more proactive four-part plan to create both financial and regulatory incentives for integrating safety into care delivery.

Institute of Medicine
Patient Safety Plan[14]

1 National Center for Patient Safety

The IOM called upon the United States Congress to create a National Center for Patient Safety in the Department of Health and Human Services' Agency for Healthcare Research and Quality (AHRQ). This Center would be responsible for establishing national safety goals, tracking progress, and researching, developing, and broadly sharing new tools and systems needed to prevent, recognize, and mitigate harm from error.

2 Mandatory & Voluntary Reporting Systems

The IOM recommended establishing a nationwide, mandatory public reporting system and encouraged the growth of voluntary, confidential reporting systems to help practitioners and healthcare organizations learn about and correct problems before serious harm occurs.

3 Role of Consumers, Professionals, & Accreditation Groups

The IOM believed public and private purchasers of health insurance, regulators, and licensing and certifying groups all had a crucial role to play in applying pressure and incentives for change.

4 Building a Culture of Safety

The IOM knew that to improve patient safety, it had to become a top priority for healthcare organizations and their leadership. It urged the adoption of standard safety principles used in other industries, from designing working conditions for safety; to standardizing and simplifying equipment, supplies, and processes; to avoiding reliance on memory.

---

14   Institute of Medicine. To Err is Human: Building a Safer Health System. Washington, DC: The National Academies Press, 2000. Donaldson MS. An Overview of To Err is Human: Re-emphasizing the Message of Patient Safety. In: Hughes RG, editor. Patient Safety and Quality: An Evidence-Based Handbook for Nurses. Rockville (MD): Agency for Healthcare Research and QUality (US); 2008 Apr. Chapter

Twenty-First-Century Efforts to Improve Patient Safety and Quality of Care

2005: The PSQIA Encourages Open Reporting

In response to the 1999 IOM report and public outcry for safer systems, the US Congress passed the Patient Safety Quality and Improvement Act of 2005 (PSQIA), which helped build a foundational understanding of patient safety challenges—a crucial first step before any meaningful improvements could be implemented.[15] PSQIA established a voluntary reporting system designed to capture detailed data around incidents, near misses, and adverse events for assessment, resolution, learning, and improvement.

The 2005 act built upon the IOM's recommendation to "break down legal and cultural barriers that impede safety" by protecting the confidentiality of personal information of both the patient and the reporting organizations and staff involved. This effort made it safe for providers to report incidents without fear of legal repercussions and to share and learn from the information needed to understand and improve the safety and quality of patient care.[16]

2008: AHRQ Implements the National PSO Program

The Agency for Healthcare Research and Quality (AHRQ)—a part of the US Department of Health and Human Services—is the leading federal agency charged with responding to the issues brought to light by the IOM's 1999 report. AHRQ is responsible for identifying and

---

15   US Department of Health & Human Services, Patient Safety and Quality Improvement Act of 2005 Statute & Rule, November 2017, https://www.hhs.gov/hipaa/for-professionals/patient-safety/statute-and-rule/index.html.

16   Institute of Medicine, To Err Is Human: Building a Safer Health System (Washington, DC: The National Academies Press, 2000).

developing the knowledge, tools, and data needed to improve the healthcare system overall and for sharing this information with healthcare professionals, policy makers, and patients so that they may make more informed decisions.[17]

As part of this effort, AHRQ in 2008 implemented the Patient Safety Organization program, a voluntary program that invites providers to share information about patient safety events, learn from those events, and ultimately improve their patient care and outcomes. This initiated the approval process and listing of the nation's first Patient Safety Organizations (PSOs).[18]

2009: Patient Safety and Quality Improvement Final Rule

The Patient Safety and Quality Improvement Final Rule, known as the Patient Safety Rule, took legal effect on January 19, 2009. The Patient Safety Rule established a framework by which hospitals, doctors, and other healthcare providers may voluntarily report information to Patient Safety Organizations, on a privileged and confidential basis for the aggregation and analysis of patient safety events.[19]

---

17   "Frequently Asked Questions," Agency for Healthcare Research and Quality, updated November 2017, https://www.pso.ahrq.gov/faq#whichagenciesimplementth.

18   "Patient Safety Rule," Agency for Healthcare Research and Quality, updated November 2017, https://www.pso.ahrq.gov/legislation/rule.

19   "Patient Safety and Quality Improvement Act of 2005." PSO. Accessed August 24, 2022. https://pso.ahrq.gov/resources/act.

Patient Safety Organizations

A Genesis[20, 21, 22]

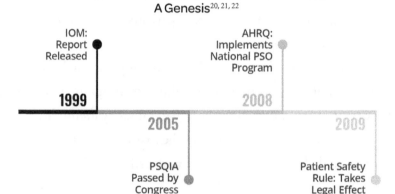

The Patient Safety Rule protects Patient Safety Work Products (PSWPs).[23] These include

- peer review documents;
- clinical practice protocols;
- staff evaluations;
- committee minutes, deliberations, recommendations, checklists, notes, or outcome data;
- equipment review logs;
- root cause analyses;
- quality and safety reports; and

20 U.S. Department of Health & Human Services, (2017). "Patient Safety and Quality Improvement Act of 2005 Statute & Rule" [Online]. Available: https://www.hhs.gov/hipaa/for-professionals/patient-safety/statute-and-rule/index.html [2017, November].

21 Agency for Healthcare Research and Quality, (2017). "Frequently Asked Questions" [Online]. Available: https://www.pso.ahrq.gov/faq#whichagenciessupplementthePSA [2017, November].

22 Agency for Healthcare Research and Quality, (2017). "Patient Safety Rule" [Online]. Available: https://www.pso.ahrq.gov/legislation/rule [2017, November].

23 "What Is a Patient Safety Work Product?," Agency for Healthcare Research and Quality, updated November 2017, https://www.pso.ahrq.gov/faq#WhatisaPatientSafetyWorkProduct.

- subjective reports, staff impressions, and/or other objective facts not part of mandatory reporting.

PSWPs may identify the providers and/or employees involved in a particular patient safety event, as well as HIPAA-protected patient data. Subject to certain specific exceptions, this information cannot be used in criminal, civil, administrative, or disciplinary legal proceedings. These protections enable the safe sharing of critical information that can be used to improve patient safety and overall population health.

In the years since then and even now, we are seeing more prioritization of incident reporting and PSO patient safety work product in healthcare environments. We are also seeing more emphasis on establishing and sustaining leadership-driven cultures and environments in which delivering safe, quality, and equitable care is a top priority and is achieved by using data from patient safety and quality programs as a means for learning and performance improvement.

> Delivering safe, quality, and equitable care is a top priority and is achieved by using data from patient safety and quality programs as a means for learning and performance improvement.

Aviation as a Model

Systemwide changes to healthcare in the twenty-first century have been modeled on well-established practices within the aviation industry. In fact, even the idea of establishing a just culture originated in the 1980s in aviation—an industry in which safety incidents can have catastrophic results—after it was recognized that the conditions for accidents were often known or suspected by people in the workplace who were afraid to speak up for fear of being reprimanded or humiliated. To counter that hesitation, the aviation industry established processes that created an atmosphere of trust in which essential safety information could be shared openly and *in every instance* learned from, and where accountability—in the absence of punishment or humiliation—became the norm.

The success of those changes has been significant. Despite a doubling of the number of worldwide flight hours over the past twenty years, the number of fatalities has fallen from approximately 450 to 250 per year. That result stands in surprising comparison to healthcare, where in the United States alone, there are an estimated two hundred thousand preventable medical deaths every year, the equivalent of almost three fatal airline crashes per day.[24] As airline pilot Chesley Sullenberger noted, "If such a level of fatalities was to happen in aviation, airlines would stop flying, airports would close, there would be congressional hearings, and there would be a presidential commission. No one would be allowed to fly until the problem had been solved."[25]

Extensive improvements in safety outcomes within the aviation industry have been attributed to the implementation of more efficient safety protocols that feature increased tracking and reporting of safety events. According to a 2018 study, "While North American commercial aviation currently enjoys a tremendous safety record, it was not always this way. A spike of accidents in 1973 caused 3,214 aviation-related fatalities. Over the past 20 years, the rate of fatal accidents

---

24   Narinder Kapur et al., "Aviation and Healthcare: A Comparative Review with Implications for Patient Safety," JRSM Open 2, no. 7 (January 4, 2016), https://journals.sagepub.com/doi/full/10.1177/2054270415616548.

25   Chesley Sullenberger, "Chesley, B. 'Sully' Sullenberger: Making Safety a Core Business Function," Healthcare Financial Management 67 (2013): 50–54.

per million flights fell by a factor of five, while air traffic increased by more than 86 percent. There have been no fatalities on a US carrier for over 12 years." [26]

Healthcare has started to borrow the following practices from the aviation industry:

1. *Checklists*

    The checklist approach has been championed in aviation as a method to improve safety and reduce risk. When it is time to prepare for a flight, pilots use a multistep checklist to confirm that the flight course, weather patterns, radio setup, special runway information, and other factors have all been taken into account to ensure the safest flight possible.[27]

    The checklist approach has the same potential to save lives in healthcare that it has in aviation by ensuring that simple standards are applied for every patient, every time. An early eight-week study of Johns Hopkins Hospital's surgical intensive care unit (ICU) demonstrated an improvement in the care team's understanding of patient care plans from 10 percent to 95 percent

    > The checklist approach has the same potential to save lives in healthcare that it has in aviation by ensuring that simple standards are applied for every patient, every time.

---

26   Claudia R. Gerstle, "Parallels between Safety and Healthcare," Journal of Pediatric Surgery 53, no. 5 (May 2018): 875–878, https://pubmed.ncbi.nlm.nih.gov/29506813/.

27   Alton K. Marsh, "Technique: Approaching the Approach," Aircraft Owners and Pilots Association, June 5, 1996, https://www.aopa.org/news-and-media/all-news/1996/june/pilot/technique#:~:text=When%20 it%20is%20time%20to,altitude%20for%20the%20missed%20approach.

just by using a daily goals checklist. As a result of teams' improved understanding of the plan of care, ICU professionals were able to reduce patient length of stay by 50 percent, from 2.2 days to 1.1 days.[28]

2. Risk Management

The aviation industry places heightened focus on ways to address risks through crew resource management—the effective use of all available resources to support safe and efficient operations by crew personnel—and threat and error management, which assumes that pilots will naturally make mistakes and encounter risky situations during flight operations.[29,30] Both strategies are aimed at minimizing risk and optimizing safety. Rather than try to *avoid* threats and errors, the primary focus of risk management is on teaching pilots to *manage* issues so that they do not impair safety.[31]

When the same concepts are applied to healthcare, leadership teams recognize that mistakes happen and attempt to foster a culture that emphasizes managing and learning from events.

3. Utilization of Technology

Beyond the aviation industry's technological improvements in equipment and aircraft design, there have also been

28   P. Pronovost et al., "Improving Communication in the ICU Using Daily Goals," *Journal of Critical Care* 18 (2003): 71–75.

29   "Crew Resource Management," Skybrary, accessed August 23, 2022, https://www.skybrary.aero/index.php/Crew_Resource_Management_(CRM).

30   "Threat and Error Management (TEM), Skybrary, accessed August 23, 2022, https://www.skybrary.aero/index.php/Threat_and_Error_Management_(TEM).

31   Gerstle, "Parallels between Safety and Healthcare."

significant strides in incident reporting technology. These advances allow aviation teams to report incidents and near misses, such as equipment malfunctions, unexpected adverse weather conditions, or loss of situational awareness by the flight crew.[32] Tracking these types of safety events over time allows risk management teams to identify areas of concern and put action plans into place for lasting improvement.

In healthcare, utilizing a technology-based incident reporting solution instead of tracking events on paper or in Excel can help organizations take a smarter approach toward identifying, addressing, and preventing risk. Electronic reporting tools make it easy to capture data through desktop, tablet, or mobile devices, which helps leadership teams quickly identify and address areas of concern. An effective reporting system is one that makes it easy for supervisors to identify areas for improvement in real time and alert the appropriate team members for follow-up action.

To the extent that solutions are customizable, healthcare organizations can more accurately track trends over time and establish action plans to prevent incidents before they occur.

By looking to the aviation industry as a guide, healthcare organizations have taken strides toward incorporating greater safety into their operations and getting closer to the goal of zero harm.

---

32   National Research Council, Improving the Continued Airworthiness of Civil Aircraft: A Strategy for the FAA's Aircraft Certification Service (Washington, DC: The National Academies Press), chap. 5, https://www.nap.edu/read/6265/chapter/5.

Meaningful Reporting

Within the healthcare industry, many organizations are just beginning—or have yet—to take a structured approach toward achieving a just culture of care, both when it comes to the adoption of processes associated with that culture and when it comes to establishing an infrastructure that, day to day, supports and fosters feedback through reporting and actively learning from the information gathered. Even organizations that do have in place the technological infrastructure to support active reporting and post-event management may not yet be analyzing information with a focus on process failures as the primary cause of incidents and near misses. For example, an incident reporting technology might be set up in such a way that it only allows a finite number of executives or high-level managers to look at its dashboards and utilize available reporting data. That arrangement might prevent information from reaching midlevel managers and team leaders—the very people whose daily practices are most likely to be affected by it.

The translation of data aggregated from the whole patient safety process might be slow or nonexistent, whereas real-time information can lead to near-real-time adjustments and to improved patient experiences, employee morale, and overall quality of care. For example, if the staff on a particular floor wanted to know about a particular observation reported, the manager might then have to ask for information from the director. The director might then have to ask the chief nursing officer to access information within the system that would allow them to determine what's happening on that floor and with the department or team they manage. When real-time data analytics and dashboards are not readily available to all levels of management, there can be a two-to-three-month lag in any meaningful data analysis.

A more effective system puts the power of the information it holds immediately into the hands of everyone for whom it's most relevant—any manager, for example, who might need to see the analytics to learn from them and make adjustments to the environment of care. What if the floor manager in the abovementioned example could see what's occurring in real time? If the key to establishing a just culture is transparency in reporting, the goal of transparency should be to put the power of useful information into the hands of the people who need it most *when* they need it most. Did the last shift conduct its huddle before disbanding? Was a fall assessment performed on the new patient in room 905? The nurse manager who steps into her shift on that floor should be able to determine these details—and gather more if she needs—from a quality rounding tool. If the information goes into the system and travels up to the chief nursing officer but never makes it back to relevant team leaders, it's not being utilized to its maximum capacity; worse, the time lapse can lead to more rather than fewer incidents occurring.

Another great opportunity that arises with improved efforts to collect and distribute patient safety and quality data is the capacity to make use of data across institutions. The modernization of patient safety technology systems allows for use of common formats in reporting. It's one thing that there are well-established common formats for those organizations that participate in Patient Safety Organizations, but when you consider that there are 6,093 hospitals in the United States and that there are over 2.5 million total points of care in the United States, it becomes clear just how many other healthcare organizations would benefit from being able to contribute and compare data across institutions.[33]

33   "Fast Facts on US Hospitals," American Hospital Association, updated January 2022, https://www.aha.org/statistics/fast-facts-us-hospitals.

The AHRQ continues to respond to these issues and improve the safety of US healthcare. Using AHRQ's research and how-to tools, the US healthcare system prevented 1.3 million errors, saved 50,000 lives, and avoided $12 billion in wasteful spending in the period from 2010–2013 alone.[34] Between 2014 and 2017, AHRQ research reduced the number of hospital-acquired conditions by 910,000, preventing 20,500 hospital deaths and saving $7.7 billion in healthcare costs.[35] What changes like these demonstrate is that when we increase access to standardized processes and tools, our healthcare organizations and teams are able to decrease incidents and prevent patient harm.

Even with the successes outlined above, our journey to zero harm continues. Ongoing voluntary and confidential reporting of safety events enables researchers to analyze data and turn that analysis into improvements in both training and care. The increased use of established common formats for collecting and sharing patient safety information makes possible comparisons among healthcare organizations to advance learning and thereby change everyday practices both within and across systems. These two shifts alone move organizations toward enacting the principles of a just culture of care. As we'll see in the next few chapters, there are still other shifts or steps to be taken, and each one of them is applicable, no matter the size or structure of a given point of care.

---

34   "Agency for Healthcare Research and Quality: A Profile," Agency for Healthcare Research and Quality, updated July 2022, https://www.ahrq.gov/cpi/about/profile/index.html.

35   "AHRQ Scorecard on Hospital-Acquired Conditions," Agency for Healthcare Research and Quality, updated July 2020, https://www.ahrq.gov/professionals/quality-patient-safety/pfp/index.html.

CHAPTER 3

Embracing
Near-Miss Reporting

Much attention has been paid to reducing medical errors. Electronic prescriptions avoid penmanship mistakes. Bar codes on wristbands ensure that medications go to the right patient. Checklists and timeouts before surgeries help prevent common oversights. But we can stop only the errors we know about. There remains a black hole of near misses, of uncharted errors—a black hole of shame that prevents caregivers from coming forward.

—Danielle Ofri, MD, PhD, clinical professor of medicine,
New York University School of Medicine

There is an entire field of study dedicated to the use of technology and predictive analytics in healthcare. This applies to tasks like monitoring and anticipating the spread of flu infections in hospitals as well as interventions for predicting the onset and slowing the progression of end-stage renal disease. Ultimately, the practice of medicine is headed in the direction of preventive care. We are headed in the same direction when it comes to patient safety, especially in the practice of capturing key information to identify risk factors before incidents occur. In chapter 1 we addressed how organizations that commit to the reporting process push through the initial, and sometime difficult, discoveries and move to awareness, learning, and ultimately to prevention. We also identified just cultures of care as ones that celebrate near-miss reporting—reporting about events or unsafe conditions that are identified before patient or employee harm occurs. By increasing the number of near misses and unsafe conditions reported, healthcare organizations gain a greater understanding of their safety challenges and prevent future harm.

In the 1930s, American engineer William Heinrich developed a model for understanding the scale and scope of "safety"—or the lack of it—in industry. His much-challenged but never-refuted Heinrich Ratio, or Heinrich Pyramid, has influenced safety programs across industries, including healthcare. Heinrich suggested that for every death or serious injury, there are approximately 29 adverse events, 300 near misses, and 3,000 latent risks creating unsafe conditions.[36]

36   Yorio, Patrick L, and Susan M Moore. "Examining Factors That Influence the Existence of Heinrich's Safety Triangle Using Site-Specific Data from More than 25,000 Establishments." Risk analysis : an official publication of the Society for Risk Analysis. U.S. National Library of Medicine, April 2018. https://www.ncbi.nlm.nih.gov/pmc/articles/PMC6238149/#:~:text=Heinrich%20proposed%20a%20 specific%20ratio,OSH%20policy%20and%20management%2C%20their.

Incident Ratio Model:
Adapted from Heinrich's Theory[37]

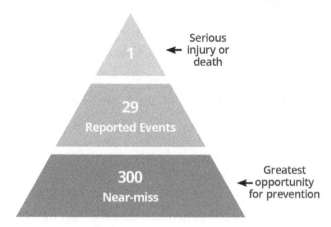

According to a study released by the US Department of Health and Human Services, roughly 86 percent of patient safety incidents occurring in healthcare organizations go unreported, with near misses underreported up to 100 times more frequently than serious events.[38,][39] Barriers to reporting—such as fear of negative repercussions, lack of understanding about what qualifies as a safety event or near miss, and the complexity of the reporting process—can all deter reporting. But for patients to receive the highest quality of care possible, reporting must become a *proactive* undertaking rather than one that collects or performs analysis only after harm occurs. Events that did not result in patient harm *but could have* are the most important data points for the prevention of future harmful incidents.

37   Leveraging the Largest Patient Safety Learning Engine. Retrieved from https://www.rmf.harvard.edu/CRICOBlog/2018/August/Leveraging-the-largest-patient-safety-learning-engine

38   Robert Lowes, "Most Adverse Events in Hospitals Go Unreported," Medscape Medical News, Medscape, January 6, 2012, https://www.medscape.com/viewarticle/756540.

39   Susan Wallace et al., "Promote a Culture of Safety with Good Catch Reports," Pennsylvania Patient Safety Authority 14, no. 3 (September 2017), http://patientsafety.pa.gov/ADVISORIES/documents/201709_goodcatch.pdf.

The *Journal of General Internal Medicine* published a meta-analysis of eight studies, which determined that over twenty-two thousand preventable deaths occur in US hospitals each year.[40] Organizations that only report incidents while not encouraging near-miss reporting are literally missing out on a valuable resource for identifying areas of safety improvement. Tracking near misses provides unique insights into an organization's safety culture and aids in measuring progress.

Here are several key benefits of tracking near-miss events:

1. **Increased Patient Safety**

    Tracking near misses provides leverage and trend data to prevent incidents before they occur. For instance, if it becomes apparent that near-miss medication errors are happening most frequently in a certain department, leadership can explore why that is and put action plans in place to prevent future errors from occurring. It may be the case that an understaffed department or shift experiences more frequent near misses or errors. By trending safety data and pinpointing near misses down to the specific department or specific shift, it is possible to identify contributing factors and prevent errors before they cause patient harm.

2. **Improved Employee Engagement and Recognition**

    Recognizing and rewarding staff can encourage near-miss submissions and provide more opportunities to improve patient safety. For example, a program at the University of Vermont Medical Center invites staff members to report near

---

40   Bill Hathaway, "Estimates of Preventable Hospital Deaths Are Too High, New Study Shows," Yale News, January 28, 2020, https://news.yale.edu/2020/01/28/estimates-preventable-hospital-deaths-are-too-high-new-study-shows.

misses using a one-page online form. The center's medication safety coordinator noted that each month the program awards one employee a $100 gift card, a "good catch" pin, and a write-up in the employee newsletter. Monthly winners are eligible for an annual prize of $500 and additional recognition in the newsletter.[41]

Near-miss programs give organizations a platform to empower frontline staff. "The frontline staff is our biggest asset," said Abigail Halloran, MA, the director of risk management and performance improvement at Haven Behavioral Health. "They see everything and know everything. The more sophisticated and proactive they become, the safer our patients are going to be."[42]

3. Data-Driven Decision Making

Utilizing tools such as customized dashboards with drill-through analytics allows healthcare teams to turn vast amounts of data into actionable decisions that drive timely results. Small-to-midsize organizations may be reassured to know researchers have found that near-miss reporting can be implemented in a variety of post-acute and ambulatory care settings to great effect, including lowering care costs and improving patient and employee satisfaction.

41   Kate Traynor, "Safety Culture Includes 'Good Catches,'" American Society of Health-System Pharmacists, September 11, 2015, https://www.ashp.org/news/2018/01/12/safety-culture-includes-good-catches?loginreturnUrl=SSOCheckOnly.

42   Susan Wallace et al., "Promote a Culture of Safety with Good Catch Reports."

Encouraging reporting to include near misses fosters a culture of care because of the following attributes:

- **Fostering a psychologically safe environment.** When staff do not feel like they have a safe, supportive environment to speak up about incidents, patient safety is likely to suffer as a result. It is the responsibility of leadership to foster an environment of physiological safety, one in which fear of negative consequences for reporting safety incidents or near misses is reduced. When staff report close calls and hazardous conditions, leaders should act quickly by addressing concerns and treating the event as an opportunity for learning, not blame.[43]
- **Emphasizing learning.** Employees must understand their specific roles and responsibilities in upholding organizational safety. Learning from near misses and minor safety issues requires analyzing data, communicating findings, and taking action. To ensure that all employees understand their roles, leadership should be sure to encourage employees and implement continuous training about how to report observations and the value that doing so brings to patients and care teams.

Anonymous Reporting

With roughly 86 percent of patient safety events in US hospitals going unreported due to fear of blame or retaliation, anonymous reporting

---

43   The Joint Commission, Sentinel Event Alert 60, December 22, 2018, https://www.jointcommission. org/-/media/tjc/documents/resources/patient-safety-topics/sentinel-event/sea_60_reporting_culture_ final.pdf?db=web&hash=5AB072026CAAF4711FCDC343701B0159.

can help organizations place the focus back on patient safety and shift from a culture of blame to a culture of encouragement—one that identifies systemic and root causes, learns from reports, and takes targeted actions to prevent future occurrences.

Anonymous reporting can increase the number of reports submitted by decreasing fear of negative repercussions and other incentives to hide information. For example, a study in the *Journal of Hospital Medicine* comparing anonymous and nonanonymous incident reporting systems showed that the reporting of medical errors was 54 percent higher with the anonymous system.[44] The study also showed that the number of near-miss reports was three times higher in the anonymous system.

> Anonymous reporting can help organizations place the focus back on patient safety and shift from a culture of blame to a culture of encouragement.

Anonymous reporting also increases awareness of safety-related information. For example, when Trinity Health, the tenth largest health system in the United States, implemented an anonymous incident reporting and reviewing system in thirty-two hospitals and four home health agencies, the result was an increase in hospital-related safety communication.[45] With reporting systems that streamline communication, organizations can improve safety awareness across departments and increase their response times.

---

44 Taylor, James, Dena Brownstein, Eileen Klein, and Thomas Strandjord. "Evaluation of an Anonymous System to Report Medical Errors in Pediatric Inpatients." https://shmpublications.onlinelibrary.wiley.com/journal/15535606, August 7, 2007. https://shmpublications.onlinelibrary.wiley.com/doi/10.1002/jhm.208.

45 Paul Conlon et al., "Using an Anonymous Web-Based Incident Reporting Tool to Embed the Principles of a High-Reliability Organization," in Advances in Patient Safety: New Directions and Alternative Approaches, ed. K Henriksen et al. (Rockville, MD: Agency for Healthcare and Research Quality, 2008), https://www.ncbi.nlm.nih.gov/books/NBK43630/.

With that said, anonymous reporting does have some drawbacks, primary among which is that anonymous reporting may lead to information gaps. To mitigate such gaps, any questions and instructions on an anonymous report should emphasize the importance of including as much detail as possible. An effective anonymous incident reporting system should have the ability to add conditional follow-up questions that are specific to the type of incident that occurred. For example, if the "patient fall" category is selected, questions specific to falls (such as patient risk and time of last fall-risk assessment) can automatically be added to the report to ensure that all relevant information is collected at the time of reporting.

Beginning a near-miss reporting program with anonymous reporting can be a way to increase reporting, at least initially. Once a culture of reporting and organizational trust is established in an organization, anonymous reporting may prove to be less important.

Learning from Reporting

A healthcare organization can invest in a best-in-class electronic reporting system; however, it will labor to get information into that system if it does not succeed at encouraging voluntary reporting and learning among its staff.

Organizations encourage reporting among staff in the following ways:

- **Lower the reporting threshold.** The great value of reporting near misses and incidents is not just that they provide organizations with a more complete picture of what risks may exist but also that they encourage even more reporting among staff. Within a culture of safety, reporting is destigmatized.

- **Clarify that all relevant factors will be analyzed.** When staff are convinced that near misses and incidents are the product of multiple factors and that *all* contributing factors will be considered during analysis, they will understand patient safety to be the responsibility of entire care systems rather than single individuals.

- **Conduct logical analyses aimed at action plans.** Thorough review of all contributing factors and underlying causes (such as understaffing, poor system design, and faulty equipment) encourages trust in the process of analysis. When action plans address relevant issues (such as increased staffing, improved systems, and the use of checklists and other protocols), an organization demonstrates its commitment to long-term results rather than short-term fixes.

- **Share the results of the process.** Key action points should be shared with clinical staff, and regular trainings should emphasize a team-based approach by outlining some incidents and discussing both their causes and changes made to prevent the reoccurrence. Reporting succeeds when results are communicated through system improvements.

- **Follow through on action plans.** When staff see visible changes and are made aware that their commitment to safety is valued, most will embrace the reporting system as a way to improve the environment in which they work and care for patients.

- **Foster a team approach.** Management can set an example by completing reports themselves and supporting those who may find it stressful to share observations. It should be clear that each member of the organization has a vital role to play, especially frontline care providers and patient intake staff who are often in positions to witness incidents and near misses that may not be noticed by management.

Prevent Harm with Near-Miss Reporting

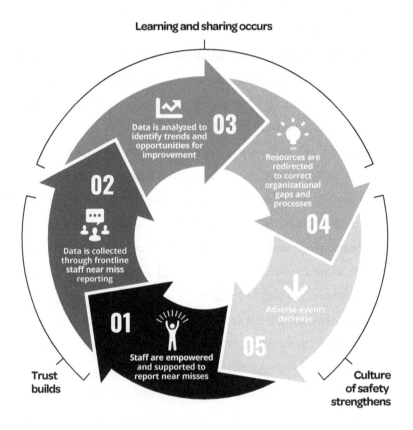

Our Pathway to Prevention

Healthcare employees operate with a significant amount of anxiety about sharing observations regarding potential harm with their organizations. Many believe that speaking up and sharing information leads to unfair reviews of themselves or their team members and does not lead to results that prevent future incidents. The reality is that what we call "never events" often begin as near misses. It is our human tendency to trend toward the safe choice, and within certain organizations, the safe choice is silence instead of speaking up. But by our silence, we are choosing to render our healthcare systems more fragile and diminish our sense of possibility for safer care delivery.

Creating and sustaining a just culture is a daily practice, not a one-time fix. Our aim as healthcare professionals is to create the safest space possible, and that involves psychological and physical spaces for learning from reported information. We know that incident reporting does not automatically alleviate harm. But when nonpunitive, objective processes are put in place, our care teams will become more actively engaged. Once we make regular reporting and follow-up part of daily work life, they take root and positively impact both employee morale and patient safety outcomes.

> When an incident occurs within a just culture, the first question asked is "What happened?" rather than "Who is to blame?"

Part II of this book, chapters 4–7, offers options for "how to" create, formalize, and strengthen event reporting and patient safety programs in our healthcare organizations. We'll consider possibilities for lowering the reporting threshold, reviewing *all* factors contributing to an event, and conducting objective analyses aimed at devising action plans and organizational learning. Part II is an overview, rather than an exhaustive study, of how the various components of a patient safety program work together to improve the quality and value of healthcare. Too often, the components of a patient and employee safety program—should one exist at all—are siloed or segmented through varying job functions or different parts of an organization.

My goal is to share with you the well-established processes for jump starting patient and employee safety practices and how to build a culture of reporting as a means of prevention. Establishing a just culture relies on a systems-thinking approach, on understanding that patient safety incidents are generally the products of faulty systems and organizational cultures, rather than solely brought about by the person or persons directly involved. When an incident occurs within a just culture, the first question asked is "What happened?" rather than "Who is to blame?" The chapters in Part II will trace the significance of that critical switch in perspective and show how event reporting fits within the larger aim of preventing harm.

Let's get started.

PART II

CHAPTER 4

Establishing a Patient Safety Committee

We must ask what is responsible, not who is responsible. The aim
of safety work is not to judge people for not doing things safely, but
to try to understand why it made sense for people to do what they
did—against the background of their engineered and psychological
work environment. If it made sense to them, it will for others too.

—Sidney W. A. Dekker, Safety Science Innovation Lab founder
and author of Just Culture, Safety Differently

I t wasn't until the Patient Safety Committee was reviewing updated
data on patient falls that the story started to become clear. At first,
the committee members did not understand why recent training on
the use of gait belts to ambulate patients failed to reduce the number
of falls. Conversations with staff and further analysis of each new fall
showed something surprising: a gait belt had not been used in many
recent falls. The reason? There weren't enough belts in the facility, gait
belts were not readily available in each patient room, and all available
belts were in use with other patients at the time of the falls. When

this came to light in a committee meeting, senior leadership quickly resolved the matter: "There are twenty rooms. Buy twenty gait belts, label each with a room number, and place one in each room."

To expect flawless performance from human beings working in complex, high-stress environments is unrealistic and will not improve safety. Humans are best guarded against errors when placed in an error-resistant *environment* where the systems, tasks, and processes they work within are well designed and the materials they need are easily available. For that reason, significant improvements in patient and employee safety begin when we focus on the environment of care that surrounds the people delivering care.

A progressive healthcare organization is one that understands that increased complexity in healthcare delivery *increases* the risk of patient safety incidents occurring. For example, a patient might receive the incorrect medication due to two medications sharing packaging similarities or because the prescription routes through multiple levels of administration, starting with the prescribing provider, then the clerk entering the order, then to the pharmacy for dispensing, and finally to the frontline care team that administers the medication to the patient. Safeguarding processes are usually in place, but an organization's safeguarding culture may relax, and lapses in the process may contribute to errors. Routinely, the frontline care provider who administered the medication would take the blame for the incident and might also be reprimanded as a result. Unfortunately, focusing solely on human factors does not allow all the factors and lapses within

> To expect flawless performance from human beings working in complex, high-stress environments is unrealistic and will not improve safety.

the system in which the incident occurred to surface. Often, multiple near misses and latent system errors occur well before an incident involves patient or employee harm.

A study conducted by the Maryland Patient Safety Center found that pairing patient safety programs with patient safety organization participation decreased preventable deaths, malpractice costs, neonatal mortality, falls with injuries, birth trauma, and worker's compensation claims. Given that preventable medication errors cost approximately $20 billion annually, improvements in this one area alone promise significant outcomes and savings for all involved.

Patient Safety Program Outcomes[46]

Preventable Deaths	Neonatal Mortality
⬇ 100%	⬇ 79%
Birth Trauma	Malpractice Cost
⬇ 74%	⬇ 56%
Falls with Injury	Worker's Compensation
⬇ 54%	⬇ 50%

The Institute of Medicine (IOM) places emphasis on patient safety by prioritizing *systems* of care delivery that

---

46   Maryland Patient Safety Center. (2012). Benefits of Joining a Patient Safety Organization. Retrieved from http://www.marylandpatientsafety.org/html/education/2012/handouts/documents/Benefits of Joining a PSO.pdf

1. prevent incidents,

2. learn from incidents that do occur, and

3. are built on cultures of safety that actively engage healthcare professionals, patients, and entire organizations.[47]

When an organization decides to ensure successful implementation of patient safety strategies, five essential ingredients are required:

- Clear policies and procedures
- Leadership engagement
- Data to drive safety improvements
- Skilled healthcare professionals
- Effective involvement of patients in patient care

In this and the chapters that follow in part II, we will review the core building blocks of patient safety programs to provide a high-level overview of how functions and roles can work together to achieve a safer environment for our patients and employees.

One essential aspect of improving patient safety, and often the first step in developing a safety program, is to establish a patient safety committee. The purpose of this committee is to *identify* patient safety trends and opportunities to develop sustainable interventions and to *promote* initiatives that improve the quality and safety of patient care.[48] In so doing, the committee helps to prevent and reduce risks, incidents, and harm that can occur during the delivery of care.

---

47 P. Aspden et al., Patient Safety: Achieving a New Standard for Care.

48 "Patient Safety Committee," Nevada Hospital Association, accessed August 23, 2022, https://nvha.net/patient-safety-committee/.

Seven Steps to Establishing a Patient Safety Committee

There are seven essential steps to establishing a patient safety committee within any size of organization. The key to establishing the committee and improving upon patient safety initiatives that currently exist is to start small—*it takes just two people to establish a committee and begin making an impact.* Those two people will determine the scope of the committee's work and its initial undertakings.

1. Enlist an Executive Sponsor

The Patient Safety Committee will require an executive sponsor, and commonly this person is a member of the organization's senior leadership. Establishing an executive sponsor is important for two fundamental reasons. First, for a patient safety committee to be effective, it must be identified as a priority by the top leaders within the organization. Staff must see this commitment to be willing to engage in patient safety initiatives themselves and trust the organization will manage information responsibly and nonpunitively. The second reason to designate an executive sponsor is to establish the investment of time and resources into the patient safety program. The executive sponsor plays a crucial role in allocating resources and making patient safety a priority when creating the organization's annual budget. When beginning a program with a committee of just two people, the executive sponsor should be one of those.

2. Determine the Appropriate Committee Size

After establishing the need for a patient safety committee and securing an engaged executive sponsor, a smaller organization may begin with one other committee member, typically a clinical leader both respected and trusted by the staff. That clinician's direct relationship with employees, patients, and systems will provide valuable insights to the committee. In general, it is important for committee members to be comfortable with uncomfortable conversations and information, as conducting challenging conversations is often key to a committee's success. Establishing a patient safety committee with fewer members allows for the committee to function sooner and increases the likelihood of establishing the capacity to address uncomfortable findings.

A chief compliance officer at a nonprofit regional health system employing forty-five hundred people across six hospitals shared with me her views on keeping the patient safety committee small to start: "We learned this the hard way. The first committee meeting included approximately twenty-five people. A few attendees shared lecture-style formal presentations, which had undertones of blame and centered around a mentality of 'we' versus 'they.' After the first meeting, we had a debrief to discuss a recent patient safety event and clarify the goals of the committee. When we regrouped, we found that the committee would be more effective with fewer members, which would give members a chance to voice their observations in a secure, open environment. This was our first crucial conversation. After it, the committee started making significant changes in the safety and care of our patients."

Designating additional committee members is a collaborative process between the executive sponsor and clinical lead. Once again, appropriate committee members are high-performing individuals who are also comfortable with challenging conversations. If the organization has many departments, the committee may evolve to include leaders from each of the following:

- Nursing/clinical care
- Quality/risk
- Pharmacy

- Laboratory
- Executive leadership
- Food and nutrition
- Physical therapy / occupational therapy / speech therapy
- Facilities management

Leaders that oversee more than one of these departments may begin by representing multiple areas within the committee. Ad hoc members will be added as needed, and their addition is driven by the nature of whatever specific initiative the safety committee is working on. Initiatives are often identified using data gathered from the incident reporting system, clinical rounding tools, and checklists. Although a representative from human resources is not considered to be a standard member of a patient safety committee, an HR representative may occasionally provide ad hoc insights and consult on employee coaching and growth. Once the committee is established, there will be times when an issue is discovered to be person related rather than process related. If necessary, HR will be able to assist by working with this employee outside of the committee setting, allowing the committee to stay focused on opportunities for improvement, rather than becoming absorbed in HR functions.

3. Select a Committee Chair

The committee chair is responsible for establishing initiatives, preparing meeting content, and coordinating schedules. This person should be as unbiased as possible. For instance, choosing someone from the organization's centralized risk or quality leadership team will allow for an organization-wide focus. Ideally, the chair will have patient care experience *and* a strong understanding of the facility or system's operational processes.

4. Set an Initial Committee Meeting Date and Agenda

After the committee members have been established, set the first meeting four weeks out. Those weeks are necessary for collecting pertinent information and preparing the agenda.

5. Review Policies and Procedures

During that preparation period, committee leads will talk with key stakeholders in patient safety to gather answers to these questions:

1. What structures and systems are in place right now that allow us to gather information about patient safety events?
2. How do we track those events, and how do we follow up on them?
3. What's working well and not working well with our patient safety efforts?
4. What are our most pressing concerns?
5. What are the most important actions we can take to improve patient safety?

Individual committee members should be asked these same questions in order to learn about their knowledge of existing processes, their access to any recorded data, and whatever anecdotal experiences they have to share. Receiving broad staff input is one of the most valuable tools available to leaders in healthcare. Staff want to know that their voices matter, that administration is listening, and that the challenges they identify will become building blocks for creating a safer environment of care. Establishing a committee without consulting staff

> Receiving broad staff input is one of the most valuable tools available to leaders in healthcare.

early on can lead to difficulties down the road, as the committee makes decisions that affect the systems and processes affecting employees' day-to-day activity.

The answers to those five initial questions will inform the very first committee meeting by providing agenda items for discussion and outlining key policies and procedures that the Patient Safety Committee will review. It is useful to offer an outline to guide discussion. Agenda items may include the following:

- Defining the scope of the Patient Safety Committee
- Determining metrics and key indicators that will be reviewed each month
- Establishing protocol for how to report incidents
- Establishing protocol for capturing near misses
- Establishing protocol for post-incident activity management
- Determining analysis tools
- Establishing a process for learning/change/improvements to occur
- Evaluating the possibility of enrolling in a Patient Safety Organization

Moving forward, the committee will want to engage in regular review of the organization's current policies and procedures to identify those that are most relevant to the committee's work and to track any changes.

6. Define and Monitor Metrics for Success

Establishing measurable goals, clear metrics, and key indicators for monthly review is key to the success of the patient safety committee. When the committee meets for the first time, it is critical to identify which metrics the committee will monitor and measure.

The safety indicators the committee chooses to measure do not have to be overcomplicated; in fact, it is better to keep them basic to start. Think about how the committee will best effect change to improve safety within the organization. The key is to start with attainable goals, identify areas for improvement, implement action plans, and then determine whether actions resulted in improved patient safety outcomes. If the metrics for success seem unattainable, the committee may experience data paralysis and delay action planning.

Tools and data for establishing success metrics include

- culture of safety scores,[49]
- employee engagement surveys,
- incident and near-miss reports,
- checklists and rounding tools, and
- annual safety risk assessments.

These, among others, are tools the committee will utilize to develop a system for reviewing incidents for severity and probability, as well as to establish relevant incident categories for monitoring, such as medication errors, falls, and patient grievances.

7. Establish Action Plans

When the committee begins to create and revise action plans, it's important to focus on strong actions and intermediate-level actions rather than weaker, more passive actions.[50]

---

49   The Agency for Healthcare Research and Quality (AHRQ) has Surveys of Patient Safety Culture for hospitals, medical offices, nursing homes, community pharmacies, and ambulatory surgery centers. You can find these surveys here: https://www.ahrq.gov/topics/surveys-patient-safety-culture.html.

50   "Guidance for Performing Failure Mode and Effects Analysis with Performance Improvement Projects," Centers for Medicare & Medicaid Services, accessed August 23, 2022, https://www.cms.gov/Medicare/Provider-Enrollment-and-Certification/QAPI/downloads/GuidanceForFMEA.pdf.

According to guidance from the Centers for Medicare & Medicaid Services (CMS), stronger actions include

- changing physical surroundings,
- usability testing of devices before purchasing,
- engineering controls into systems that force the user to complete an action,
- simplifying a process to remove unnecessary steps,
- standardizing equipment or processes, and
- ensuring that leaders are seen, heard, and actively involved in making and supporting changes on behalf of patient and employee safety.

Intermediate actions include

- increasing staffing and decreasing workload,
- enhancing/modifying software,
- eliminating/reducing distractions,
- utilizing checklists and other cognitive aids,
- eliminating look-alike and soundalike terms,
- utilizing "read backs" to ensure clear communication, and
- enhancing documentation and communication.

Weaker actions include

- double checks;
- warnings and labels;
- new procedures, memoranda, or policies;
- training or in-service; and
- additional study or analysis.

The primary aim is to establish actions that clearly support staff in their day-to-day work. In the words of an executive sponsor on her patient safety committee experience: "A learning curve for our team was understanding that most action plans contain weak actions, rather than strong and intermediate actions. When the action plan is complete, go back and evaluate each action to determine whether it is strong, intermediate, or weak. Then reassess the plan to determine whether there are enough of each category of action. Keep in mind that you want the staff to be successful, so ensure that the action plans set out by the patient safety committee don't set the staff up to fail—meaning, don't make it more difficult for them to take care of patients and get their jobs done. Sometimes actions are so complicated the staff won't be able to comply, and they will develop work arounds to fit their own processes for patient care."

Though there is much to process in the initial meetings of the Patient Safety Committee, the goal is to establish a procedure that, generally speaking, will govern meetings from that point forward. Some parts of the procedure may change—development and refinement are ongoing—but committee meetings will establish a regular rhythm. When that occurs, an agenda like the following might be used.

Sample Patient Safety Committee Agenda

MEETING TITLE:	Patient Safety Committee	DATE & TIME:	Insert Date & Time
FACILITATOR:	Insert Name	LOCATION:	Insert Location
EXECUTIVE SPONSOR:	Insert Name	NEXT MEETING:	Insert Date & Time of Next Meeting
RECORDER:	Insert Name		
PURPOSE:	A patient safety program encompasses all the means by which healthcare organizations protect their patients from errors, injuries, accidents, and infections.		
ATTENDEES			
Insert Name	Insert Name		

Insert Name	Insert Name		
Insert Name	Insert Name		
Insert Name	Insert Name		
Insert Name	Insert Name		
AGENDA TOPICS			
Topic	**Person**	**Time**	**Discussion Items**
Call to Order	Committee Lead	1 min	
Approval of Prior Meeting Minutes	Team	5 min	
Review of Metrics	Committee Lead	10 min	
Review of New Incidents	Team	10 min	
Review of Root Cause Analyses Performed	Team	20 min	
Review of Action Plans in Progress	Team	20 min	
Education	Committee Lead / Topic Expert	10 min	
Policies & Procedures	Team	5 min	
Adjourn			

Building Organizational Trust

A Patient Safety Committee is created to promote safe, quality health-care by identifying opportunities and promoting evidence-based best practice standards. To achieve its goals, the committee works collaboratively to establish organizational trust.

As leaders in our healthcare organizations, we can help instill in everyone a sense of personal responsibility by establishing trust, clear expectations, and psychologically safe environments—those in which there is no fear of negative consequences for reporting information. When staff report near misses and hazardous conditions, leaders can directly and quickly address concerns so that measurable improvements in safety emerge.

Every year, the Joint Commission receives reports from healthcare staff of unsafe conditions in their organizations. The majority of these reports indicate that leadership had not been responsive to these concerns or to other early warnings.[51]

Our first step toward organizational safety is starting the conversation in the committee. The beginning will not be perfect; however, that initial heavy lift will lighten when we understand employees, patients, and leaders to be active parts of creating change. Each one of us must become part of the evolutionary process in which protecting lives is considered important enough to set aside any stigmas and negativity around reporting. Our goal is to embrace reporting as an opportunity for learning and a chance to pay forward what we learn by actively participating in preventing harm. The front lines of medicine are staffed by people who care enough for others that they willingly acknowledge the actions, environmental issues, and other circumstances that threaten patient safety and who have the courage to share their observations so that we can reduce the shame and silence that surrounds patient and employee safety work in our healthcare systems.

---

51   The Joint Commission, Sentinel Event Alert.

CHAPTER 5

Building an Effective Reporting System

A standardized reporting system is a necessary tool for

reaching proactively toward a culture of prevention.

Adrian routinely entered incidents into the incident reporting system for the sixty outpatient laboratory sites and hundreds of phlebotomists he managed. His staff also logged hundreds of incidents a month, but Adrian was not able to see data about the incidents that would allow him to pinpoint which ones were occurring at which sites or identify trends that might lead to process improvement and staff retraining: "We were logging incidents and near misses, but I couldn't see higher-level data or analysis of that information that I could use to make improvements. I'm a manager, but within the software system, I had no access to data trends or other summary reports to assist me with pinpointing the quantity, type, shift, and locations of the occurrences."

It wasn't until his quarterly meetings with leadership that Adrian would learn what was going on within his own department. The information would be delivered to him as a reprimand: "Adrian, you had a hundred and thirty-seven reports this week alone! And why didn't you write up these four employees with repeated incidents?" Eventually, Adrian and other managers raised the issue of needing access to the same level of data that leadership accessed.

Adrian's organization ultimately needed to invest in an entirely different incident reporting system that allowed user-level access to data analytics and dashboards. That allowed each manager to run reports and access data belonging to the departments they managed. Once the organization invested in new software, Adrian and his colleagues were able to access near-real-time reporting and analytics. "Seeing my department's data organized on dashboards allows me to manage system or process breakdowns in nearly real time. Now I can quickly follow up and make changes that have a positive, and sometimes immediate, effect on patient and employee safety."

> Modernizing patient safety technology systems across all points of care is paramount.

According to the Joint Commission—a US-based nonprofit healthcare evaluation and accreditation organization—patient safety programs that include incident, event, and near-miss reporting "are a mainstay of efforts to detect patient safety events and quality problems." The Joint Commission requires all hospital members to maintain a voluntary incident reporting system and accredits more than twenty-two thousand US healthcare organizations and programs.[52] But given that there are over 2.5 million points of care in the United States

---

52 "History of the Joint Commission," The Joint Commission, accessed December 17, 2020, https://www.jointcommission.org/about-us/facts-about-the-joint-commission/history-of-the-joint-commission/#:~:text=Founded%20in%201951%2C%20The%20Joint,the%20highest%20quality%20and%20value.

alone, most of those care centers currently depend on patient safety and quality programs created in house or on paper, require manual entry of information, and lack data analytics tools for spotting trends. Modernizing patient safety technology systems across all points of care is paramount; electronic platforms have become necessary tools for guiding users through standardized processes of data gathering, aggregation, and analysis for change.

A straightforward and accessible electronic user interface for submitting events increases the value of the reporting system and the ease of use for broad groups of healthcare personnel. An electronic software system provides a common language for reporting, and with input from clinical staff, it can be customized to include prompts that make the reporting of event details even clearer and more meaningful to both reporters and reviewers. These technology systems also generate and promptly disseminate reports that can be used to analyze and prioritize events and track progress on system changes enacted to prevent harm.

Patient safety technology supports healthcare organizations in their efforts to prevent patient safety events and can yield the following outcomes:

Benefits of Patient Safety Technology

1. **Closer to zero harm.** With standardized reporting tools (as well as clinical rounding tools and checklists that both reduce complexity and standardize processes), a healthcare team can deliver safer, higher-quality care.

2. **Coordinated care.** Consistent and coordinated care across a team of providers is necessary for ensuring patient safety, avoiding preventable

Closer to Zero Harm

Coordinated Care

Patient Engagement

Standardization

Continuous Learning

patient harm, and meeting patients' needs and preferences. A centralized technology hub for team collaboration eliminates the departmentally siloed approach to assessing safety and quality indicators.

3. **Patient engagement.** Patient involvement in their own care is recognized as a key component in the advancement of patient safety. As far back as 2007, the Joint Commission mandated that healthcare organizations "encourage patients' active involvement in their own care as a patient safety strategy," catalyzing research into how patients may inadvertently hasten incidents as well as how they may partner with providers to prevent them.[53]

4. **Standardization.** Technology-enabled checklists and common format templates have played a major role in patient safety movement successes. The algorithmic listings of actions to be performed in a given clinical setting, for example, ensure that every step is followed for every patient every time, thereby reducing the risk of behavioral slips on the part of the care team.[54]

5. **Continuous learning.** One of the most powerful ways a patient safety technology leads to performance improvement is by helping providers identify and leverage trend data to prevent incidents before they happen. When providers have a platform for easily capturing, analyzing, and sharing data—either exported to registries and organizations like PSOs (which facilitate data aggregation and benchmarking across facilities) or shared internally with staff and executives—providers can proactively address potentially harmful situations and minimize escalation.

---

53 "Patient Engagement and Safety," Patient Safety Network, updated September 7, 2019, https://psnet.ahrq.gov/primer/patient-engagement-and-safety.

54 Agency for Healthcare Research and Quality, Checklists, January 2019, https://psnet.ahrq.gov/primers/primer/14/Checklist.

Key Characteristics of an Effective Incident Reporting Program

Voluntary incident reporting is utilized to record individual cases of adverse events or near misses. From the reporting of these individual cases, there are two methods to identify safety hazards retrospectively: (a) the screening of large databases for evidence of preventable events, and (b) analysis of individual cases. In response to individual cases, patient safety personnel may conduct more in-depth reviews such as root cause analyses and mortality reviews.

An effective healthcare incident reporting program has the following characteristics:

- The *privacy* of staff who report occurrences is protected within a supportive institutional culture.
- Reporting tools are *accessible* to all staff, and reports are received from a broad range of personnel.
- Summaries of reported events are appropriately disseminated and reviewed for *timely follow-up* actions.
- Structured mechanisms are in place for reviewing reports along with developing, implementing, and following up on *action* plans related to identified safety hazards.[55, 56]

A reporting program that relies on a dedicated electronic platform has distinct advantages over those based on disparate software systems or spreadsheet- and email-based methodologies. A single, comprehensive platform provides guidance to a broad range of staff in real time,

---

55   "Patient Safety Primer," Patient Safety Network, Agency for Healthcare Research and Quality, accessed November 30, 2018, https://psnet.ahrq.gov/primers/primer/13/Reporting-Patient-Safety-Events.

56   J. C. Pham et al., "What to Do with Healthcare Incident Reporting Systems," Journal of Public Health Research 2, no. 3 (December 1, 2013): e27, https://www.ncbi.nlm.nih.gov/pmc/articles/PMC4147750/.

and it uses a common language to describe events, common data points for analyzing events, and common prompts that direct staff to include specific details associated with an event. A comprehensive electronic platform makes it easy to generate and disseminate reports in a timely manner so that system changes can be implemented quickly. Finally, a comprehensive platform gives patient safety personnel the ability to tie action plans to identified safety hazards and then analyze the effectiveness of those plans.

> A standardized reporting system is a necessary tool for reaching proactively toward a culture of prevention.

A standardized reporting system is a necessary tool for reaching proactively toward a culture of prevention. For small to midsize healthcare facilities, using an event reporting technology that is developed for simplicity and speed of reporting can affect whether or not a report is completed and submitted. A study in the *Journal of Public Health Research* (*JPHR*) recommends the following strategies to maximize the value of electronic event reporting systems across various types of healthcare facilities:

- Make reporting easier.
- Make reporting meaningful to the reporter.
- Make the measure of success system changes rather than events reported.
- Prioritize which events to report and examine, report and examine them well.
- Convene with diverse stakeholders to enhance the value of the incident reporting system.[57]

---

57   J. C. Pham, et al., "What to Do with Healthcare Incident Reporting Systems."

Today's leaders in healthcare provision are taking a farsighted approach to handling day-to-day operations and addressing risk by implementing incident management software that allows managers and leaders at all levels to identify trends and minimize time spent retrieving data from disparate sources.[58]

To achieve those goals, keep the following parameters in place when designing a system or systems:

- **Simplicity.** Design simple and concise incident and event intake reporting forms. If a form is long and complicated, people will be reluctant to complete it.

- **Accessibility.** Ensure that reporting forms are easily available on all computer terminals and devices across all areas of the organization. This can be accomplished by adding a user-friendly icon allowing for one-click access into the patient safety system.

- **Confidentiality.** Ensure that the forms can be submitted confidentially or anonymously and sent confidentially and immediately to the corresponding management group so that staff members can be assured that the information they provide is kept private.

- **Trust.** A culture of trust is vital to encouraging regular reporting. For an organization to improve safety long term, staff members must trust leadership and management not to assign blame unfairly or focus solely on human factors. Similarly, leadership and management must trust their teams to exercise due diligence and identify and report information that may affect safety.

---

58   Yasser K. Alotaibi and Frank Federico, "The Impact of Health Information Technology on Patient Safety," Saudi Medical Journal 38, no. 12 (December 2017): 1173–1180, https://www.ncbi.nlm.nih.gov/pmc/articles/PMC5787626/.

Selecting a Reporting Software: Start with the End Result in Mind

The patient safety committee has the initial task of assessing current processes, resources, and tools within an organization. From those findings, the committee determines the essential information that it intends to collect, keeping in mind the type of healthcare organization, the ways in which workflow and processes are organized, and the core types of incidents that occur. The next step is to identify a patient safety technology tool, which includes information intake (reporting) as well as post-event activity management, root cause analysis, follow-up action plans, data analytics, and dashboards.

It is essential that incident reporting systems provide a complete workflow tool that will manage events from intake to resolution and system-wide actions for process improvement. For organizations that currently have patient safety technologies in place, the information in this section can be used to review existing systems and determine whether features meet the goals of the patient safety committees.

Incident reporting systems are significant financial investments for institutions, so it is vital that they provide the infrastructure and process workflows to support a highly effective patient safety program. Stavropoulou et al. conducted a systematic review, including forty-three studies comparing incident reporting systems and their impact on "improving patient safety through organizational learning."[59] Their findings showed that the most successful incident reporting systems contained *explicit guidance on what counts as an incident*, "were owned and led by clinical teams rather than centralized hospital departments, and ... were embedded within organizations as part of wider safety

---

59 C. Stavropoulou et al., "How Effective Are Incident-Reporting Systems for Improving Patient Safety?," Milbank Quarterly 93, no. 4 (December 2015): 826–866.

programs."[60] Remember, the overall aim when designing a reporting system is to determine whether incidents that are considered important are being reported, and then to determine whether those reports are useful for changing structures or procedures to avoid or mitigate such incidents in the future.[61]

A patient safety committee determines the types of events that may occur in an organization and determines the data to capture in reports by considering what the organization aims to learn from the information it collects. When an organization begins with these ends in mind, it is more likely to design event reporting forms to capture data that will be useful for identifying trends and deploying limited resources, such as human time for activity management, resources for training, or system redesign. Depending on an organization's needs and capacities, reporting can be tailored for committee review and/or departmental measures, dashboards can be built for both high-level and drill-down reporting, and data analytics can be configured to track and analyze trends by type of incident, location, time of day, shift, and other contributing factors. Patient safety systems route reports, communications between committee members and teams, and associated documentation to the relevant people and allow for collaborative actions and follow-up to be tracked in one centralized repository. Systems with automatic processes and communication tools built in allow for the information collected to be shared in close to real time.

It is important to remember that a reporting tool is not just a receptable for capturing data but also an intuitive system that coordinates, analyzes, and directs information, and manages activity. For

---

60   C. Stavropoulou et al., "How Effective Are Incident-Reporting Systems?"

61   Paul Wiele, "Healthcare Incident Reporting: The Impacts of Usability of Input Interfaces, Usability of Resulting Data, and Attitudes Towards Reporting" (thesis, Rochester Institute of Technology, 2016), https://scholarworks.rit.edu/theses.

example, in a well-designed and well-implemented technology tool, when an incident or near miss is initially reported:

1. The reviewers and any relevant management or leadership are automatically alerted that an event has been received and is ready for review.
2. Communication, documentation, analysis, and action plans are managed and assigned to team members through a centralized channel and repository, allowing for timely team communication.
3. Built-in escalation processes, with automatic reminders and alerts, keep team members on track and informed about next steps.

Fundamental Features of Reporting Software

Usability covers a number of software functions, from being designed in such a way as to encourage people to complete forms to collecting information that provides a thorough understanding of incidents, from being sharable to making sense to those whose responsibility it is to aggregate and analyze reports.

When evaluating software solutions for incident management, the patient safety committee will look for the following features:

1. Accessible

An efficacious software solution will be readily accessible and easy to launch and navigate. Staff should know exactly where to go to report an incident or near miss.[62] In software development, we gauge ease of

---

62   Stanford Medicine, Stanford Medicine Health Trends 2017 Report: Harnessing the Power of Data in Health, June 2017, http://med.stanford.edu/content/dam/sm/sm-news/documents/StanfordMedicine-HealthTrendsWhitePaper2017.pdf.

use and user experience by the number of clicks it takes to complete a process. Initiating and submitting a report should take fewer than three clicks. Select a platform designed and developed in a way that makes complex processes look and feel simple yet includes the ability to collect data points on all fields in the form *and* guide the user through standardized processes, from initial reporting to action plans to learning. Submitting a report should be as simple as walking to the nearest computer terminal or device, clicking on a button to open an event report, and finding distinctive icons for each type of event that is typically reported within the organization. For example, a staff member reporting a fall will click on a button with a distinct image representing falls.

> Select a platform ... that makes complex processes look and feel simple yet includes the ability to collect data points on all fields in the form.

The software will also include tooltips for greater efficiency. A tooltip is a text description that is displayed when a user hovers the cursor over an icon or image.[63] For example, a tooltip for reporting a medication incident might feature relevant subcategories like adverse reaction, delay, and look alike / soundalike. Utilizing features like tooltips enables staff to quickly determine the proper course of action for reporting various types of incidents.

---

63   Alita Joyce, "Tooltip Guidelines," Nielsen Norman Group, January 27, 2019, https://www.nngroup.com/articles/tooltip-guidelines/.

2. Customizable

It is essential to choose a solution that is customizable to an organization's specific needs. An effective patient safety solution is adaptable to existing processes; in other words, the system should not require an organization to change its processes to meet the technology's capabilities. For example, if an organization uses the term "location" instead of "facility," then the questions on an intake form should reflect that language to make it understandable for staff.

Likewise, a technology solution should be adaptable to the evolving field of patient and employee safety, as well as the findings and recommendations of the patient safety committee, by offering the ability to add or remove questions from a report or to create new forms. Given that an effective reporting software should allow team members to complete incident reports in fewer than three minutes, organizations should look for the ability for users to complete the reporting forms by using radio buttons, drop-down boxes, and contingency questions instead of free text fields, which tend to be more time consuming.

To achieve accurate data-driven decision making, healthcare managers must carefully consider the reporting capabilities offered by a particular software solution. For instance, can the system generate drill-through reporting (such as tracking patient falls by department, location, time, and care team), or is the solution limited to analyzing data only on a macrolevel? Also consider whether reports can be converted into multiple file formats and whether the system features the capability to export data. The goal is to capture as many key facts as possible in the shortest amount of time. Team members should feel that they can file a report and quickly return to patient care.

3. Interoperable

Having a single platform with accessible data allows care teams to stay informed and engaged. A software solution for reporting and risk management should securely integrate with electronic health records to simplify the process of pulling patient information, resulting in faster reporting time.[64]

Technology companies have made progress in interoperability; however, we still have a way to go. Not all technology vendors have developed—or will allow—interoperability with other vendors. Developing a single platform usually requires a given healthcare organization's insistence on and advocacy for achieving interoperability between vendors' systems.

4. Centralized Communication Portal

A patient safety committee should look for a solution that offers automatic routing to the person(s) or team responsible for initiating post-reporting activity management. For example, if an incident or near miss occurs in the infusion center, that department's supervisor(s) will be notified immediately. However, if what is reported in this case is a medication error, the pharmacist will also be notified for follow-up.

Organization-specific routing protocols are customized during software implementation, and each healthcare organization will have a unique routing schema that is built into its technology. Patient and employee safety technology fosters clearer and more transparent communication between leadership, care providers, and patients. Having a single platform with communication tools allows users real-time

---

64   Shane Whitlatch, "The 5 Key Benefits of Healthcare Interoperability," Becker's Health IT, Becker's Hospital Review, February 27, 2018, https://www.beckershospitalreview.com/healthcare-information-technology/the-5-key-benefits-of-healthcare-interoperability.html?oly_enc_id=2071D010994514Q.

access to information and a centralized repository for storing details and tracking trends. This capacity increases the efficiency of resolution and allows risk managers to quickly identify high-risk areas.

5. Real-Time Dashboards with User-Specific Access

When safety events are displayed through data visualization tools such as a graph or pie chart, it allows risk and quality leaders to view trends and generate follow-up action plans.[65] These visual tools are useful for leadership as well as all levels of management; a tool that allows users to access dashboards and analytics according to their specific security levels is best. User-friendly dashboards give managers the ability to track trends over time, identify areas of improvement, and proactively reduce risk. Access to real-time information helps providers identify exactly where incidents and near misses are happening, allowing leadership teams to strengthen their interventions and processes for preventing future safety events before they occur.[66]

Imagine staff members making the effort to report an event, only to find the task time consuming, confusing, or difficult to submit. Recall the situation within Adrian's organization—he was able to submit reports but could not access data analytics that would allow him to make productive changes within the work environments he managed. Given that encouraging near-miss reporting is the goal of a proactive safety culture, a reporting system must be both intuitive and fast.

---

65   Robert Hanscom, "Variation in Healthcare Delivery: The Need for Standardization," Becker's Health IT, Becker's Hospital Review, February 15, 2018, https://www.beckershospitalreview.com/healthcare-information-technology/variation-in-healthcare-delivery-the-need-for-standardization.html.

66   Yasser K. Alotaibi and Frank Federico, "The Impact of Health Information Technology on Patient Safety."

Building Electronic Event Reporting Forms

When designing incident and near-miss reporting intake forms, the first goal is for healthcare teams to submit reports with the click of a few buttons, allowing them to spend less time on administrative tasks and more time on patient care. Healthcare teams can benefit from general changes in web form design. Recent advances in the design of web forms in applications have increased the rate of completion of those forms by up to 40 percent.[67] Changes emphasize prompting for key details rather than encouraging more open-ended responses.[68]

Building reports to encourage detailed information intake requires attention to the following:

- **Build for your healthcare setting.** The information organizations most need to collect depends on their type: acute-care settings have different needs from post-acute, ambulatory, or social services. Common Formats have yet to be created for most types of organizations, but it is possible to find software platforms specifically suited for specific care settings.
- **Capture core information for spotting trends.** Typical information includes the date and time of the event, name or anonymous identifier, location or department where the event occurred, job function of the person involved, and the type and brief description of event and any observers.
- **Adhere to common categories.** To the extent possible, use common core data points for reports and common report schemas.

---

67   L. Wroblewski, Web Form Design: Filling In the Blanks (New York: Rosenfeld Media, 2008).

68   U. Pettersson, "Improving Incident Reports in the Swedish Armed Forces" (unpublished doctoral dissertation, Lund University, Lund, Sweden, 2013).

1. Comply with Web-Form Guidelines

An empirical study performed by Google of existing user experience guidelines for web form design concluded that improved web forms lead to faster completion times, fewer form submission attempts, and increased user satisfaction.[69] According to the study, a well-designed reporting form meets the following general criteria:

- Form content—Forms should be short and intuitively ordered, allow flexibility in answers, and clearly distinguish between required and optional questions.
- Form layout—Fields for answers should be labeled above, listed one per row, and sized appropriately for the length of the answer.
- Input types—Menus, checkboxes, buttons, or open response fields are appropriate for different numbers and types of answers. Options should be in an intuitive order and limited in number if possible.
- Error handling—Answers should have their expected formats clearly indicated and should not be cleared by errors. Error messages should be polite, informative, embedded in the form, and easily noticed.
- Form submission: Submission buttons should only be usable once and not be confusable with "reset" buttons. Submissions and how they will be used should be confirmed.

---

69   Mirjam Seckler et al., "Designing Usable Web Forms—Empirical Evaluation of Web Form Improvement Guidelines" (CHI 2014 presentation, Toronto, Ontario).

2. Identify Event Types

The Agency for Healthcare Research and Quality (AHRQ) is responsible for developing Common Formats for the reporting and analysis of patient safety data. AHRQ's Common Formats are a set of standardized definitions and configurations that make it possible to collect, aggregate, and analyze uniformly structured information about patient safety for local, regional, and national learning.[70] The Common Formats give providers proven templates and guidelines to improve patient safety and quality within their organizations.

The effort to create and optimize Common Formats is ongoing and continues to develop as the industry evolves.[71] To date, AHRQ has developed Common Formats for three major settings of care—hospitals, community pharmacies, and skilled nursing facilities. The AHRQ Common Formats include the following:

- A common set of definitions of patient safety concerns that may give rise to patient harm and examples of patient safety reports
- Paper forms for versions prior to CFER-H V2.0 to guide the development of data collection instruments
- A users' guide, which describes how to use the formats
- A metadata registry with data element attributes and technical specifications for use by developers[72]

To encourage widespread adoption and learning, AHRQ's Common Formats are available in the public domain. With that said,

---

70   "Understanding Patient Safety Confidentiality," US Department of Health & Human Services, updated June 16, 2017, https://www.hhs.gov/hipaa/for-professionals/patient-safety/index.html.

71   "Understanding Patient Safety Confidentiality," US Department of Health & Human Services.

72   Overview. PSO. (n.d.). Retrieved August 24, 2022, from https://pso.ahrq.gov/common-formats/overview

organizations will want to select events and categories most relevant to their needs, many of which may exceed the categories available through AHRQ.

AHRQ Common Formats for Event Reporting (CFER) define three types of events:

1. **Near misses:** "Close calls" are patient safety events that did not reach the patient. An example of a near miss is a bed rail that is left in the unlocked position while occupied by a patient, but the patient does not fall from the bed as a result. These are the most common event types, accounting for 41 percent to 61 percent of known reported incidents.[73]

2. **Adverse events:** "Occurrences," or what we've been calling "incidents," are safety events that reached the patient, whether or not there was harm involved. An example of an incident is a patient fall.

3. **Unsafe conditions:** These are circumstances that increase the probability of a patient safety event occurring. An example of an unsafe condition is a defective bed rail that is not repaired.

The circumstances that cause near misses are not substantially different from incidents that cause actual patient harm. Given that near misses are much more prevalent and more numerous than adverse events, organizations that encourage near-miss reporting will have a larger data set to analyze than ones that only look at incidents to understand the circumstances that can lead to harm.

73   S. G. Marchon et al., "WV Jr. Patient Safety in Primary Health Care: A Systematic Review," Cadernos de Saúde Pública 30, no. 9 (September 2014): 1815–1835, doi:10.1590/0102-311x00114113.

Incidents and Relative Frequencies[74]

3. Identify Core Data Points

To analyze large amounts of data in a meaningful way, event intake forms must be built and implemented in a standardized format. For all events, there are common data points that need to be collected; these detail the type of patient safety concern, the circumstances of the event or unsafe condition, patient information (if applicable), and reporter information. The following data points are built into every event form.

A. Circumstances of the Event

- Date and time of event
- Location of event (e.g., lab, procedure room, waiting room, pharmacy, etc.)

---

74   Wiele, Paul, "Healthcare Incident Reporting: The Impacts of Usability of Input Interfaces, Usability of Resulting Data, and Attitudes Towards Reporting" (2016). Thesis. Rochester Institute of Technology.

- Contributing factors (e.g., communication, data issues, environment, staff qualifications, supervision/support, etc.)
- Narrative description of event or unsafe condition

B. Patient Information

- Identifying information about the patient affected (e.g., date of birth, age range, sex, ethnicity, race)
- Degree of harm to the patient (e.g., adverse event, near miss)
- Duration of harm to the patient (e.g., permanent or temporary)

C. Reporter Information

- Job or position (e.g., healthcare professional, healthcare worker, emergency service professional, patient, family member, volunteer, caregiver, etc.)

4. Determine Event Categories

The Patient Safety Committee will determine the most common types of events that occur within an organization. For example, common incidents and events for an FQHC might include falls, medication, injury, diagnostics, environmental concerns, security issues, compliance, employee safety, and patient relations. Behavioral health centers might have special categories such as restraint/seclusion, self-harm, and elopement. And LTACs might prioritize infection, equipment, dietary, pressure ulcers, and the like.

Healthcare facilities may have all or a handful of common event categories:

Common Event Categories

Near Miss	A near miss can be included in all of the categories listed here; however, including an accessible button making near misses a stand-alone category of their own will encourage reporting as well as allow for the ease of reporting of this rich information that drives prevention.
Falls	Assisted, unassisted
Medication	Incorrect medicine, look alike / soundalike, med rec, pharmacy
Compliance	Abuse, behavior, appropriateness of care, HIPAA
Security	Aggressive/disruptive behavior, building not secure, property loss/ damage
Patient Relations	Communication, humaneness/caring, institutional issues, patient rights, quality, safety, security, timing and access, billing
Employee Safety	Exposure, injury, abuse
Infection Control	Pneumonia, COVID-19, bloodstream infection, surgical site infection, precautions
Equipment	Broken equipment, electrical shock, equipment malfunction, equipment not cleaned, lost equipment
Environment of Care	Cleanliness, biohazardous waste, equipment, supplies, facility, trash, event
Exposure	Airborne, needle stick, sharp injury, splash/spill
Unanticipated Event	Missed order, emergency response, environmental emergency, left AMA, readmit within thirty minutes, unplanned transfer
Injury	Bump, bruise, abrasion, fracture
Diagnostics	Incorrect test, notification delay, contaminated specimen
Surgery/Procedure	Accidental puncture, delay/cancellation, return to surgery, wrong patient, wrong site
Mother/Baby	Delayed delivery, injury, code transfer, precipitous delivery, newborn code
Assessment	Wrong protocol, wrong assessment

5. Determine Data Points Specific to Each Category

Each type of event will have a unique question set and specific data points collected to identify trends. An incident report schema for a common occurrence—patient falls—might look like the following:

Fall Report

General

Date of Event

Time of Event

Name of Employee
Last Name, First Name

Location/Department Where Event Occurred

  ○ East Facility   ○ South Facility
  ○ North Facility   ○ West Facility

Type of Person Involved

  ○ Patient

    Last Name, First Name

    FIN/MRN

    Date of Birth

Type of Fall

  ○ Assisted   ○ Unassisted

Fall Outcome

  ○ Death: patient died as a result of the fall
  ○ Major: resulted in surgery, casting or traction
  ○ Minor: resulted in application of dressing, ice, cleaning of wound, etc.
  ○ Moderate: resulted in suturing, steri-strips, fracture or splinting
  ○ None/ no apparent injury

What was the most severe injury sustained by the Individual as a result of the fall?

(If more than one, check the most severe)

○ Bruise/abrasion   ○ Sent to hospital

○ Crushing injury   ○ Skin tear

○ Dislocation   ○ Sprain/strain

○ Fracture   ○ Swelling

○ Intracranial injury   ○ N/A

○ Laceration requiring sutures

Where did the fall occur?

○ Bathroom   ○ Patient room

○ Facility grounds   ○ Other: _____

○ Hallway

What was occurring during the fall?

○ Ambulating   ○ Reaching

○ Changing positions   ○ Showering

○ Dressing or undressing   ○ Therapy

○ Fell out of bed   ○ Toileting

○ Fell out of chair/ wheelchair   ○ Transferring

○ Other: _____

Was a fall risk assessment conducted prior to the fall?

○ Yes   ○ No   ○ N/A   ○ Unknown

Was the patient on fall prevention protocol at the time of the fall?

○ Yes   ○ No   ○ N/A   ○ Unknown

Fall Risk Factor(s)

Check all that apply:

- ○ Alone at time of fall
- ○ Attempting to toilet alone
- ○ Confused
- ○ Dizziness/syncope
- ○ Generalized weakness
- ○ History of falls
- ○ Sedated/medicated
- ○ Other: _____

Was the individual on new medication known to increase the risk for a fall when the fall occurred?

○ Yes   ○ No   ○ N/A   ○ Unknown

Were restraints in use at the time of the fall?

○ Yes   ○ No   ○ N/A   ○ Unknown

Brief Description of Incident:

Location/Department Where Event Occurred

○ Yes

> Please provide first name, last name, contact information, date and time of notification for all individuals notified.

○ No   ○ N/A   ○ Unknown

Was there a witness to the event?

○ Yes

> Please provide first name, last name, contact information, date and time of notification for all witnesses.

○ No   ○ N/A   ○ Unknown

Organizational Accountability

Over the years, my colleagues and I have noticed the differences between organizations that implement reporting systems without addressing organizational culture as compared with organizations that implement systems and approach the information collected in a non-punitive way—essentially adopting a just culture of care. In the latter, we noticed and were repeatedly told by staff about reductions in anxiety around reporting and a decrease in hypervigilance. But there was something even deeper at play in these healthcare organizations. For some, it was as if the entire organization—leaders, managers, and care-givers alike—had experienced a profound therapeutic effect. Individuals talked about colleagues within the organization as their partners on a journey to safeguard both patients *and* employees. When I first started hearing these types of remarks, I thought, *We have to understand this, and we, as a technology company, need to develop more tools to support the evolution of patient safety and quality-of-care initiatives.*

> I thought, We have to understand this, and we, as a technology company, need to develop more tools to support the evolution of patient safety and quality-of-care initiatives.

That's what we did. We participated in focus group sessions with healthcare organizations within varying care verticals—thirteen different provider types (skilled nursing, home health, government managed health providers, etc.)—and after nearly each session, we came back to the development team with an innovation. Some of these innovations were simple, others more complex. The data we collected after implementing those innovations either assured us that we should stay the course or encouraged us to change directions until we identified a more effective solution. We weren't surprised when some of the simplest applications of technology became the ones that most empowered healthcare teams. As we'll see in the next chapter, when used in a setting in which everyone is actively working to create a just culture of care and support patient safety, technology-based reporting systems promote accountability and facilitate the journey to zero harm.

CHAPTER 6

Post-Event Follow-Up

System thinking is a discipline for seeing wholes. It is a framework
for seeing interrelationships rather than things, for seeing
"patterns of change" rather than static "snapshots."

—Peter Senge, American Systems scientist and senior
lecturer, MIT Sloan School of Management

There had been several instances of healthcare professionals arriving late to assist with a code blue in the ICU. Each of these incidents was reported in the patient safety system, though no harm had come to any patient from the delayed arrivals. Each incident had also been reviewed and then closed out as "in need of no further action." Because the hospital used a reporting system with built-in data analytics, the system identified a correlation among the different cases. Each time a person had been late, they had relied on the hospital's primary elevators to get to the ICU. Once this similarity was tagged, analysis revealed that the elevators were unreliable—they were often slow and occasionally out of order, and in one case, several staff members were momentarily trapped when the elevator stopped between floors. When the root cause was discovered—the elevators were preventing staff from quickly getting to where they needed to be—the solution was clear: the hospital needed to invest in new elevators immediately.

In prior chapters, we've emphasized the great value of reporting near misses and unsafe conditions in addition to actual patient and employee safety incidents. Given that data from near misses or hazardous conditions is used for proactive identification of trends and prevention of harm, as reporting these becomes the norm in an organization's culture, the more likely it is that incidents with harm will decrease. Earlier we learned that near misses in healthcare occur up to one hundred times more frequently than serious incidents.[75] Reporting them is critical to preventing harm.

What Happens after an Event Is Submitted?

The different levels of event review are determined by the individuals engaged in the review process: departmental managers are typically the first to engage in review, followed by quality and risk managers, and later, if determined necessary, root cause analysis (RCA) teams, and possibly peer review and/or mortality review teams. The patient safety committee will often be involved in reviewing incidents resulting in patient harm. At each level, the report is either closed out or escalated to the next group of reviewers.

For example, if an organization is using technology tools for reporting, once an event is submitted, it will be routed to the appropriate manager or managers. These managers gather information to document what happened and identify all contributing factors, and they will assign a severity level to the event. From there, a report will be reviewed by a quality or risk manager, who may also add to the file or follow up with those involved for greater clarification. Most events

---

75   Susan Wallace et al., "Promote a Culture of Safety with Good Catch Reports."

are closed at this point or after any recommended follow-up actions, policy changes, or trainings have occurred. The data gathered from each submission will be aggregated and used to identify trends across all submissions that can help focus prevention efforts.

Severity categories within an organization may vary, but general categories include *low* (no harm or minimal harm), *moderate* (short-term harm), *severe* (long-term or permanent harm), and *fatal*. These may also be tracked by level of injury, as in *near miss*, *no injury or unaffected*, *minor injury*, *major injury*, and *death*. Following the categorizations in the following chart, levels three through five would all require RCA.

Outcome Severity Rating Scale[76]

Rating	Outcome Category	Description
5	Catastrophic	Resident experiences death or major permanent loss of function (sensory, motor, physiologic, or intellectual).
4	Major	Resident experiences permanent lessening of bodily function (sensory, motor, physiologic, or intellectual), disfigurement, surgical intervention required, or increased level of care for 3 or more days.
3	Moderate	Resident experiences an event, occurrence, or situation which could harm the resident but will not cause permanent injury or lessening of bodily function or require the delivery of additional healthcare services.
2	Minor	Resident may experience a minor injury, but most likely would not be affected by the failure and it would not cause any change in the delivery of care.
1	Near miss	Resident would not experience any injury, changes in delivery of care, or an increased level of care.

It can be just as effective (and perhaps less intimidating) to have the team rate outcomes using descriptive terms such as:

- **Low** (minimal resident harm)
- **Moderate** (short-term resident harm)
- **Severe** (permanent or long-term resident harm)

---

76   Centers for Medicare & Medicaid Services. (2014). Guidance for Performing Failure Mode and Effects Analysis with Performance Improvement Projects. Retrieved from https://www.cms.gov/Medicare/Provider-Enrollment-and-Certification/QAPI/downloads/GuidanceForFMEA.pdf

Communicating with Patients and Families

When an incident with patient harm occurs, healthcare leaders can choose to take an approach referred to as "delay, deny, and defend" or meet the challenge with organizational accountability. Communication and Optimal Resolution (CANDOR) is an AHRQ-funded toolkit that highlights an organization's accountability for its clinical outcomes by emphasizing transparency in patient interactions and candor to rebuild trust after an event.[77] Instead of engaging in denial and defense of organizational procedures and individual practitioners, CANDOR requires that organizations provide immediate emotional first aid to patients, families, and caregivers; that ongoing communication is maintained; that just and timely resolution takes place; and that patients, caregivers, and families understand how care will be made safer as a result.

> CANDOR requires that organizations provide immediate emotional first aid to patients, families, and caregivers; that ongoing communication is maintained; that just and timely resolution takes place.

The MedStar Health Institute for Quality and Safety—an organization that partners with patients, families, and caregivers to reduce preventable harm—is one example of a comprehensive patient safety program that includes CANDOR. Established by MedStar Health, the largest healthcare provider in Maryland and the Washington, DC region, the MedStar Health Institute for Quality and Safety provides

---

77 The AHRQ CANDOR toolkit is available at https://www.ahrq.gov/patient-safety/capacity/candor/index.html.

a global infrastructure for leaders, frontline caregivers, patients, and family members to jointly develop, educate, assess, and advocate for patient safety and clinical quality initiatives.[78] Incorporating CANDOR into its processes produced the following results.

Patient Safety

- A 12 percent increase in event reporting
- A twenty-seven-fold increase in event reviews
- A 74 percent reduction of serious safety events

Medical Liability

- A 55 percent decrease in total medical liability costs
- A 42 percent decrease in claims
- A 47 percent decrease in lawsuits[79]

Not only does the incorporation of CANDOR into follow-up processes *engage* patients and families instead of *avoiding* the communication and disclosure of information, but the CANDOR process implements meaningful care for providers involved in events.[80]

Four Essential Questions to Answer during Follow-Up

Employees, patients, and caregivers who report incidents should have confidence that their concerns are heard and addressed by leadership and that their reporting had a positive effect on safety—not only by

---

78 "MedStar Health Institute for Quality and Safety," MedStar Health Institute, accessed August 23, 2022, https://www.medstarhealth.org/innovation-and-research/institute-for-quality-and-safety.

79 "What Is CANDOR?," MedStar Health Institute, accessed August 23, 2022, https://www.med-starhealth.org/innovation-and-research/institute-for-quality-and-safety/services-and-expertise/what-is-candor.

80 To access the AHRQ Communication and Optimal Resolution Toolkit, visit https://www.ahrq.gov/patient-safety/capacity/candor/modules.html.

leading to changes in care processes but also by changing staff attitudes and knowledge.[81] Post-event management involves four primary actions to ensure that processes for following up carry forward the tenets of a just culture of care.

Step 1. The first step of post-event follow-up answers the question "Who needs to be notified?"

Besides direct managers and supervisors, clinical leaders and executive teams may also receive initial notification based on the severity of the event. In the case of major injury or death, entire teams may be notified immediately.

Step 2. The next step answers the question "Why did it happen?"

In this step, care teams gain a deeper understanding of what factors contributed to the event and see exactly where improvements are necessary. Contributing causes are in no way limited to human factors. Findings in a recent study substantiate the effort to examine all factors: among the patient safety incidents reviewed, 590 contributing factors were identified, with 35 percent related to the care process, 22 percent to the healthcare environment, 13 percent to technical factors, and 30 percent to human factors.[82] Given the variety of factors that can contribute to an incident, step 2 is often the most involved part of the process, including everything from data collection and information gathering to event and trend analysis. This step includes

81   Janet Anderson et al., "Can Incident Reporting Improve Safety? Healthcare Practitioners' Views of the Effectiveness of Incident Reporting," International Journal for Quality in Health Care 25, no. 2 (April 2013): 141–150, https://academic.oup.com/intqhc/article/25/2/141/1855001.

82   M. Chaneliere et al., "Factors Contributing to Patient Safety Incidents in Primary Care: A Descriptive Analysis of Patient Safety Incidents in a French Study Using CADYA (Categorization of Errors in Primary Care)," BMC Family Practice 19 (July 19, 2018), https://bmcprimcare.biomedcentral.com/articles/10.1186/s12875-018-0803-9.

the documentation of actions and next steps, including changed processes, additional training or retraining, and the like.

Step 3. The third step answers the question "What can we learn?"

This step is critical for supporting and sustaining a just culture. Post-event review processes should identify lessons that can be shared either with the employees involved in the event or—especially in cases of more complex issues—with entire care teams.

Step 4. Step 4 answers the question "How can it be prevented in the future?"

Prevention involves implementing and following up on action plans, revising existing policies and procedures, or securing in place new procedures to improve outcomes in the future. Even those incidents and near misses that are closed out after initial review contribute data to prevention through the identification of trends.

The entire four-step process can be completed once or multiple times, depending on incident type and severity. Some incidents and events will require additional follow-up to understand what happened and to more clearly determine how to prevent similar events from occurring in the future. Events that are ranked at higher severity levels and during which patient harm occurred will be escalated for RCA—a process by which contributing system factors are thoroughly identified, analyzed, and often changed. If the RCA process is required, it is assigned to a team that could include physicians, supervisors, staff, and safety and quality improvement specialists. This team will have fundamental knowledge of the specific area involved, and none of them will be involved in the case under review. A typical RCA ranges between one and three months, with length of time often dependent on case complexity. After completion of analysis and recommendations for specific actions, the event file will either be closed or recommended for peer review or mortality review processes. The three major review processes are distinguished as follows:

- **Root cause analysis.** RCA "is a structured method used to analyze serious adverse events" in healthcare. The RCA process improves patient care by identifying breakdowns in the systems that increase the likelihood of a harmful event.[83]
- **Peer review.** Peer review is the standardized process by which healthcare providers evaluate one another's performance. The effects of environmental systems and processes remain in consideration during peer review, but emphasis is placed on drawing distinctions among human behaviors in three primary categories: human error, at-risk behavior, and reckless behavior.
- **Mortality review.** Mortality review is, as the name suggests, a process by which practitioners and teams review a patient safety event that resulted in death, permanent harm, or severe temporary harm and then implement action plans for prevention.

A Deeper Look at Root Cause Analysis

Identifying contributing factors in process design was a concept originally used in the field of engineering. The ubiquitous term *user-centered design*, for example, was coined by Donald Norman in the late 1980s. This technique "prioritizes the relevant characteristics of a user throughout the design of a product or system"[84] and entails a

---

83   "Root Cause Analysis," Patient Safety Network, Agency for Healthcare Research and Quality, accessed August 7, 2019, https://psnet.ahrq.gov/primers/primer/10/root-cause-analysis.

84   M. M. Searl et al., "It Is Time to Talk about People: A Human-Centered Healthcare System," Health Research Policy Systems 8, no. 35 (2010), https://health-policy-systems.biomedcentral.com/articles/10.1186/1478-4505-8-35).

search for *system vulnerabilities* rather than individual human errors and other *less actionable* root causes.[85] Originally, the technique was used in high-risk industries—not only airlines but the military and nuclear power industries as well.

An RCA entails the same type of search and is conducted to avoid sources of bias. It repeatedly delves into the chain of causes until it has clearly identified those at the very origin. It attempts to identify any and all vulnerabilities within systems and processes that might have contributed to an incident, and it determines where a redesign or restructuring of systems and processes could decrease the likelihood of similar events occurring in the future.[86]

The determination of all contributing factors through RCA—including the ongoing addition of relevant facts and details—requires a psychologically and physically safe, blame-free environment for sharing observations on reported incidents. Additional layers of analysis should be met with the same—or greater—levels of transparency as the initial gesture of reporting. When done effectively, an RCA will clearly identify factors that contributed to the occurrence of an incident so that specific measures can be put in place to address those factors, improve patient safety, reduce future incidences, and reduce the costs associated with risk.

It is critical to set up a structured framework for conducting RCAs and not rely on ad hoc processes. Ideally, an organization will utilize a standardized system to assist and guide the multifaceted follow-up process as well as to ensure that it occurs in a timely manner.

---

85   D. M. Oppenheimer, "Spontaneous Discounting of Availability in Frequency Judgment Tasks," Psychological Science 15 (2004): 100–105, doi: 10.1111/j.0963-7214.2004.01502005.x.

86   Sentinel event policy and procedures. The Joint Commission. (n.d.). Retrieved August 24, 2022, from https://www.jointcommission.org/resources/patient-safety-topics/sentinel-event/sentinel-event-policy-and-procedures/#:~:text=The%20Sentinel%20Event%20Policy&text=A%20sentinel%20event%20is%20a,intervention%20required%20to%20sustain%20life

In an intuitive software system, reviewers are informed of steps in the RCA process and reviewer communications by automatic alerts and notifications on their system dashboards. Dashboards give reviewers a complete list of RCA activities, the current status of each of those activities, and information about who needs to complete which activity next. Automatized tracking of the review process ensures that there is a centralized channel for team communication, thereby eliminating knowledge gaps that occur when information is exchanged via email chains. Built-in escalation processes keep team members on track and informed about next steps.

An RCA considers common patterns both of human behavior and of systems in which those behaviors take place, all with the goal of identifying problems and generating solutions.[87] When asking, "Why?" an RCA identifies key contributing factors, which can include the equipment, processes, people, materials, environment, or management—any systems and processes that might contribute to an explanation. A systems-thinking approach toward RCA requires that an effort be made to identify fundamental factors contributing to an incident and to locate any and all points in the process at which an intervention could reasonably be implemented to deliver an improved outcome and prevent harm. An RCA—and a just culture generally speaking—places emphasis on

> An RCA—and a just culture generally speaking—places emphasis on trust, learning, and positive change, rather than on assigning blame and maintaining the status quo.

---

87   M. M. Searl et al., "It Is Time to Talk about People."

trust, learning, and positive change, rather than on assigning blame and maintaining the status quo.[88]

Common Root Cause Categories and Subcategories

- **Anesthesia care:** Planning, monitoring, and/or discharge
- **Assessment:** Adequacy, timing, or scope of; assessment; pediatric, psychiatric, alcohol/drug and/or abuse/neglect assessments; patient observation, clinical laboratory testing; care decisions
- **Care planning:** Planning and/or collaboration
- **Communication:** Oral, written, electronic, among staff, with/among physicians, with administration, with patient or family
- **Continuum of care:** Access to care, setting of care, continuity of care, transfer of patient, and/or discharge of patient
- **Health information technology related:** Administrative/billing or practice management system; automated dispensing system; electronic health record, including CPOE, CDS, or eMAR; human interface device (e.g., keyboard, mouse, touch screen); incompatibility between devices; hardware failure problem; failure of or problem with wired or wireless network; ergonomics; security, virus, or other malware issue; unexpected software design issue
- **Human factors:** Staffing levels, staffing skill mix, staff orientation, in-service education, competency assessment, staff supervision, resident supervision, medical staff credentialing/privileging, medical staff peer review, other (e.g., rushing, fatigue, distraction, complacency, bias)
- **Information management:** Information management needs assessment, confidentiality, security of information, definitions, availability of information, technical systems, patient identification, medical records, aggregation of data

---

88   T. Diller et al. "A Human Factors Approach to Root Cause Analysis" (symposium presentation, December 11, 2012).

- **Leadership:** Organizational planning, organizational culture, community relations, service availability, priority setting, resources allocation, complaint resolution, leadership collaboration, standardization (e.g., clinical practice guidelines), directing department/services, integration of services, inadequate policies and procedures, noncompliance with policies and procedures, performance improvement, medical staff organization, nursing leadership
- **Medication use:** Formulary, storage/control, labeling, ordering, preparing/distributing, administering, and/or patient monitoring
- **Nutrition care:** Nutrition care planning, timing, storage, and/or patient monitoring
- **Operative care:** Operative care planning, blood use, and/or patient monitoring
- **Patient education:** Planning education, providing education, effectiveness of education
- **Patient rights:** Informed consent, participation in care, end-of-life care, pain management, privacy
- **Performance improvement:** Improvement planning, design/redesign testing, design/redesign measurement, data collection, data analysis, improvement actions
- **Physical environment:** General safety, fire safety, security systems, hazardous materials, emergency management, smoking management, equipment management, utilities management
- **Rehabilitation:** Rehabilitation care planning, patient monitoring
- **Special interventions:** Special intervention planning, assessment, restraint equipment, patient monitoring
- **Surveillance, prevention, and control of infection:** Sterilization/contamination, universal precautions[89]

---

89   The Joint Commission, Office of Quality and Patient Safety, Sentinel Event Data: Root Causes by Event Type, 2004–2015 (PowerPoint presentation).

Key Steps of an RCA[90,91]

To summarize, an RCA follows steps that mirror the four essential questions guiding all event follow-up:

1. **Identify the incident.** This involves an initial review of the incident report, follow-up documentation, and clinical documentation to understand the basics of what happened.

2. **Organize a review team.** This team should include professionals with fundamental knowledge of the specific area of concern. The team leader or facilitator should be unbiased, and team members should be treated as equals. The review team should not include members from the department where the incident occurred. The ideal facilitator would have no prior knowledge of factors of the event; possess a clear understanding of the purpose, process, and outcomes of an RCA; hold credibility within the organization; and have skills in quality improvement. In many cases, the Patient Safety Committee is likely to be the interdisciplinary team organizing the review team.

3. **Gather the facts to create a timeline.** Fact gathering should enable team members to describe the processes leading to the event. Flowcharts, story maps, and other cause-and-effect diagrams are useful. The team will conduct interviews with all involved, observe and record the "typical" process, and thoroughly review all clinical documentation relevant to the event.

---

90   Katherine Jones et al., "Conducting Individual Root Cause Analysis in Small Rural Hospitals" (Power-Point slides, University of Nebraska Medical Center).

91   Ryan Charles et al. "How to Perform a Root Cause Analysis for Workup and Future Prevention of Medical Errors: A Review," Patient Safety in Surgery 10, no. 20 (2016).

4. **Identify root causes.** Understanding what happened should include descriptions of how specific causes led to specific effects that increased the likelihood of the incident. The team discusses all factors contributing to the incident. The key to this step is using causal statements. For example: Why did the patient lose his balance? *Because he had nothing to hold on to.* Why did the patient have nothing to hold on to? *Because he was unable to locate his walker ...*

5. **Develop action plans.** From the identification of root causes, the team will identify risk reduction strategies and system improvements and may even implement a trial of planned interventions.

6. **Monitor effectiveness of changes / measure outcomes.** Outcome measurements help ensure the appropriate implementation of actions and interventions. Effectiveness should be monitored and evaluated over time and actions tweaked as necessary in light of findings.

7. **Communicate results.** Communication of results should extend beyond those immediately involved in the incident. Depending on the specific case, the CANDOR method may be followed to achieve a fair and optimal resolution for the patient, family, and health providers.

Best Practice Model: RCA²

To standardize and improve the effectiveness of the RCA process, the National Patient Safety Foundation assembled a group of experts to examine best practices for conducting RCAs with the goal of preventing future harm. In 2015, the RCA process was renamed Root Cause Analysis and Action, or RCA² (RCA "squared") to ensure that efforts result in the appropriate and timely implementation of sustainable, systems-based improvements.[92] The foundation's publication is frequently used by healthcare organizations as a guide on how to conduct effective RCAs.

The RCA² process clarified specific activities, beginning with defining which events and near misses are worthy of further review by using a risk-based prioritization system so that staff can credibly determine which hazards should be addressed first. Severity category rankings include additional factors such as the extent of the injury, length of stay, level of care required, and estimated costs. For instance, an event that required surgical intervention would be considered a higher priority than an event that only required first aid treatment—and would be escalated to the risk management team or patient safety committee for further review. RCA² also requires that staff members are educated on the importance of reporting incidents, events, and near misses and receive training on the appropriate process for doing so.[93]

> The more quickly actions are implemented, the less risk there is for additional patient injury to occur.

The RCA² process clarifies guidelines for follow-up actions, including setting task deadlines and assigning the person responsible for completing each action item. The more quickly actions are implemented, the less risk there is for additional patient injury to occur. Active participation by organizational leadership is also explicitly

92   "RCA2: Improving Root Cause Analyses and Actions to Prevent Harm," Patient Safety Network, June 24, 2015, https://psnet.ahrq.gov/issue/rca2-improving-root-cause-analyses-and-actions-prevent-harm.

93   "RCA2: Improving Root Cause Analyses and Actions to Prevent Harm," Patient Safety Network, January 2016, https://www.med.unc.edu/ihqi/wp-content/uploads/sites/463/2018/07/RCA2-National-Patient-Safety-Foundation.pdf.

embedded into the review process through a series of meetings and interviews. RCA² also emphasizes the need to have an interdisciplinary team conducting the review process in order to bring diverse perspectives to the table.

In RCA², and once the root causes of each incident are clear, the team is required to evaluate each preventive action selected. When developing these actions, organizations are encouraged to consider more specific questions, such as the following:

- What safeguards are needed to prevent this incident from happening?
- What would have to go wrong to have an incident like this happen? How can we prevent this from going wrong?
- How could we change the way we do things to make sure that this incident never happens?
- If an incident like this happened, how could we quickly catch and correct the problem before a patient ended up being harmed?
- If a patient were harmed by the recurrence of this incident, how could we minimize the effect of the incident on the patient's condition?

The strongest corrective actions are those that focus on designing controls into the system that create safeguards for preventing harm in the future. The feasibility and costs associated with actions must also be considered. Once processes are optimized, it is important that mechanisms are put in place to maintain quality going forward.[94]

RCA² emphasizes the importance of leaders sharing information regarding incidents as well as sharing the results across the entire

---

94   "What Are Common Root Cause Analysis (RCA) Tools?" 6Sigma.us, accessed August 7, 2019, https://www.6sigma.us/gsa/.

organization results and any recommendations for safety improvements so that all can learn from them.[95, 96, 97] In addition to sharing the results and recommendations of an RCA, organizations are expected to provide the resources and funding to implement the interventions for prevention that are recommended by the analysis. As we have noted, when personnel see that these action plans are fully implemented, they are more likely to buy into sharing observations, reporting events, fully participating in the RCA process, and developing a positive perception of the patient safety culture of the organization.

> The strongest corrective actions are those that focus on designing controls into the system that create safeguards for preventing harm in the future.

Tools for Conducting Root Cause Analyses

The following tools are frequently used when conducting RCAs.

Five Whys

This tool is used to get to the root cause of a straightforward problem that does not necessitate the use of advanced statistics.[98] The team will ask the question "Why?" at least five times. This allows the team

---

95   "Joint Commission Outlines 11 Tenets of a Safety Culture," Risk Management News, accessed August 3, 2019, https://www.ecri.org/components/HRCAlerts/Pages/HRCAlerts030817_Joint.aspx.

96   "Root Cause Analysis," Patient Safety Network, Agency for Healthcare Research and Quality, accessed August 7, 2019, https://psnet.ahrq.gov/primers/primer/10/root-cause-analysis.

97   "Get to the Root Cause of the Matter," presentation.

98   "11 Tenets of a Safety Culture," The Joint Commission, accessed August 3, 2019, https://www.jointcommission.org/assets/1/6/SEA_57_infographic_11_tenets_safety_culture.pdf.

to approach the root cause of the problem, because answers to the "Why?" questions are interrelated.[99]

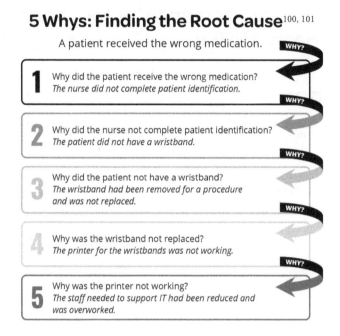

5 Whys: Finding the Root Cause[100, 101]

A patient received the wrong medication.

1 Why did the patient receive the wrong medication?
The nurse did not complete patient identification.

2 Why did the nurse not complete patient identification?
The patient did not have a wristband.

3 Why did the patient not have a wristband?
The wristband had been removed for a procedure and was not replaced.

4 Why was the wristband not replaced?
The printer for the wristbands was not working.

5 Why was the printer not working?
The staff needed to support IT had been reduced and was overworked.

Fault Tree Analysis

This tool involves the creation of a diagram that takes the shape of a tree, in which potential causes are depicted as branches.[102] Boolean logic, using the terms *and*, *or*, or *not*, is applied to each potential cause

---

99 "What is Boolean Logic?," Lotame, accessed August 10, 2019, https://www.lotame.com/what-is-boolean-logic/.

100 "Patient Safety Essentials Toolkit," Institute for Healthcare Improvement, accessed August 23, 2022, http://www.ihi.org/resources/Pages/Tools/Patient-Safety-Essentials-Toolkit.aspx.

101 Tenets of a Safety Culture, The Joint Commission. Retrieved on August 3, 2019 at https://www.jointcommission.org/assets/1/6/SEA_57_infographic_11_tenets_safety_culture.pdf

102 P. Foster, "5 Root Cause Analysis Tools for More Effective Problem-Solving," Beacon Quality, accessed August 7, 2019, https://www.beaconquality.com blog/5-root-cause-analysis-tools-for-more-effective-problem-solving.

to identify the root cause of the problem. This tool is generally used for complex processes.[103]

Fault Tree Depicting The Root Causes of Hazard to Patients During Surgery

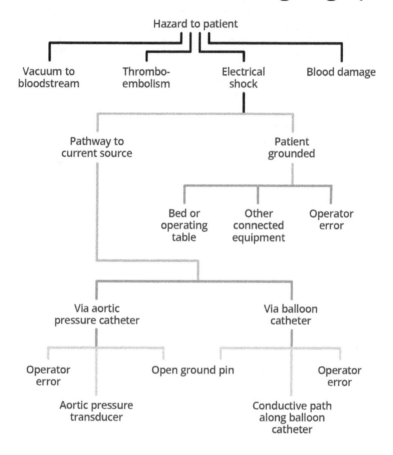

Fishbone Diagram

The shape of a fishbone is used to group potential root causes into different subcategories, such as methods, measurements, and materials

---

103   "Communication and Optimal Resolution (CANDOR)." AHRQ, accessed October 19, 2019, from
      https://www.ahrq.gov/patient-safety/capacity/candor/index.html.

for easier determination of the cause. This tool can be used to determine the root cause in complex processes.[104]

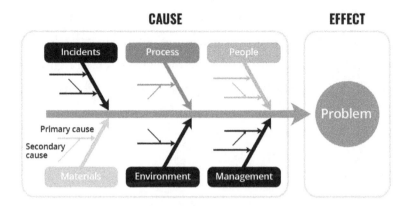

Scatter Plot or Scatter Diagram

This is a quantitative method of determining whether two variables are correlated. This tool is often utilized in combination with the fishbone diagram to test potential root causes.[105]

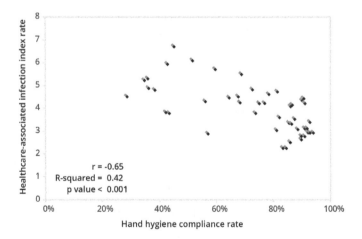

104 "11 Tenets of a Safety Culture," The Joint Commission.

105 "What Is Boolean Logic?," Lotame.

Pareto Chart

A bar chart combined with a line graph is used to group the frequency or cost of different problems to show their relative significance. The bars show frequency or cost in descending order, while the line shows cumulative percentage or total as you move from left to right. Organizations utilize this tool when they want to show the frequency of problems occurring within a process or the costs associated with the breakdown of the process.[106]

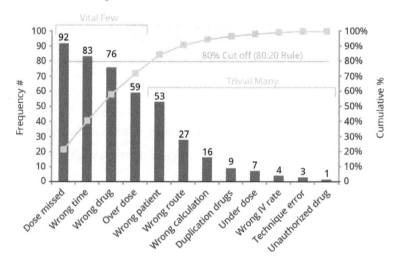

Failure Mode and Effects Analysis (FMEA)

Healthcare organizations use this RCA tool to identify which parts in a process are faulty so they can be corrected. FMEA determines the number of times a failure occurs, the actions implemented by the organization to streamline the process to prevent the failure from recurring, and whether interventions to improve the process were effective. Many organizations use this tool every time a new process is initiated.[107]

The FMEA tool prompts teams to review, evaluate, and record the following:

- Steps in the process
- Failure modes (What could go wrong?)
- Failure causes (Why would the failure happen?)
- Failure effects (What would be the consequences of each failure?)

Further Analysis

Peer Review

Clinical peer review is the dominant method of event analysis in US hospitals by which healthcare providers evaluate one another's performance to ensure that quality care standards are being met. Although peer review is a critical element of improving patient safety and quality, the model that has prevailed in the healthcare industry over the past thirty years leaves room for improvement when it comes to improving quality outcomes.[108]

According to a study published in the *American Journal of Medical Quality*, data from 296 acute-care hospitals shows that "inadequate peer review programs and related organizational factors can explain up to 18 percent of the variation in standardized measures of quality and patient safety." The study finds that most peer review programs rely on an "outmoded and dysfunctional process model" and that peer

---

107   "What Are Common Root Cause Analysis (RCA) Tools?," 6Sigma.us.

108   M. T. Edwards, "A Longitudinal Study of Clinical Peer Review's Impact on Quality and Safety in US Hospitals," Journal of Healthcare Management (2013), https://www.ncbi.nlm.nih.gov/pubmed/24195344.

review programs utilizing current best practices have "the potential to significantly improve patient outcomes."[109]

Given that the peer review process is triggered by an incident in which human factors are identified as a contributing factor, one might think of peer review as placing emphasis solely on the human factor. But the emphasis on practitioner decision making still requires investigation into *all contributing factors*. The two do not operate separately from one another, as human factors are often a reflection of the way systems are designed and function.

Peer reviews aimed at establishing and sustaining a just culture of care place greater emphasis on open dialogue and psychological safety, on ensuring that we learn from incidents, and on achieving a greater understanding of all the contributing factors, including systemic ones. Additionally, to increase the chances of unbiased assessment, peer reviews should be conducted by providers within the same specialty and, optimally, providers who are not associated with the person under review.

When implementing a process for peer review, healthcare organizations do well to focus on the following three factors:

1. **Create an open, fair, and trusting environment.** Fairness and trust in the review process require assembling a review panel of peers familiar with the procedures and processes being reviewed as well as committed to objectively consulting current literature, clinical guidelines, and hospital policy and examining multiple perspectives to ensure thorough assessment and offer systematic improvements. Objectivity during the review process should be matched by transpar-

109   Marc Edwards, "The Objective Impact of Clinical Peer Review on Hospital Quality and Safety," American Journal of Medical Quality 26, no. 2 (March–April 2011): 110–119, https://www.ncbi.nlm.nih.gov/pubmed/21169223.

ency in information sharing. Review processes can build trust through teamwork and by contributing to measurable improvements that help change existing norms and patterns for the better.

2. **Put processes in place for effective communication.** According to the American Academy of Family Physicians, "the end product of peer review should be improvement of patient care through clinician education and health system improvement. The process of peer review should seek to identify potential systematic improvements that the organization could implement to reduce the chances of mistakes or adverse events in the future."[110] Having a central channel for team communication during the peer review process helps ensure that the process proceeds in a consistent and timely manner. The patient safety committee also assists teams with the peer review process—communicating, documenting, sharing, and archiving information.

Conducting regular peer reviews allows organizations to share important information and lessons with the right people at the right time. Many conclusions reached through peer review are confidential, so disseminating this information, "often involves a degree of generalization and teaching but is critical if the peer review process is to have the intended effects of improving quality of care and patient safety."[111]

---

110   "Peer Review," American Academy of Family Physicians, accessed August 23, 2022, https://www.aafp.org/about/policies/all/peer-review.html.

111   Susan Kreimer, "Peer Review Done Right Benefits Patients, Physicians and Organizations," American Association for Physician Leadership, accessed August 23, 2022, https://www.physicianleaders.org/news/peer-review-done-right-benefits-patients-physicians-and-organizations-.

3. **Promote learning.** As healthcare organizations restructure their peer review processes, leadership teams are facilitating a shift from a punitive culture to a supportive environment that encourages performance improvement.[112]

Clinicians being reviewed should be coached and monitored to improve techniques and skills if competencies need to be addressed, and broader learnings should be shared as appropriate and used to design or redesign systems to manage behavioral choices in the future. Sharing best practices and strategies for improvement is one way of ensuring that learning takes place outside of the limited number of people involved in a given review.

When done correctly—by encouraging objectivity, putting processes in place for effective communication, and instilling a level of psychological safety that holds space for information sharing—peer review can positively impact safety and quality outcomes in healthcare.

Mortality Review

A sentinel event—any patient safety event that results in death, permanent harm, or severe temporary harm with intervention required to sustain life—triggers a mortality review.[113]

Clinicians who have training in quality standards will perform initial case review and prepare select cases for presentation to a mortality review committee. The committee then conducts a systematic review of each case brought before it to determine whether

---

112   Susan Kreimer, "Peer Review Done Right Benefits Patients, Physicians and Organizations."

113   "Sentinel Event Policy and Procedures," The Joint Commission, accessed August 23, 2022, https://www.jointcommission.org/resources/patient-safety-topics/sentinel-event/ sentinel-event-policy-and-procedures/.

and which follow-up actions are required. Support and commitment from administrators, physician leadership, and nursing leadership is paramount, as is meaningful follow through from within these groups. All participants in the mortality review process must know that they are contributing to positive change.

Before implementing mortality reviews, organizations should ensure the following:

- There is a multidisciplinary review committee so that examination of individual cases takes place from a holistic perspective.
- A tool or tools are selected that are compatible with organization type and capacity.
- All involved understand that there may be unforeseeable implications.
- All involved acknowledge the potential intensification of existing power dynamics (e.g., uneven relationships between leadership, physicians, nurses, and the frontline care team) when a patient death has occurred.
- There is a commitment to the accurate documentation of distinctions between factors that can and cannot be changed, and commitment at the highest levels to objective process completion.[114]

---

114 Marcia Rachel and Mary Stewart, "Establishing a Mortality Review Process," Journal of Nursing Care Quality (February 2009), doi:10.1097/01.NCQ.0000345538.36713.1c.

It is equally important to review patient injuries and deaths that are *not* associated with sentinel events. Doing so provides useful information about a facility's capabilities that should be prioritized for targeted improvements. The identification of trends is paramount in the shift toward harm prevention. As with other review processes, actions taken should be assessed at reoccurring intervals to ensure adherence to desired outcomes.[115]

Improvements in review processes emphasize the systemic turn toward learning, improving quality, reducing risk, and preventing harm. In root cause analyses, as in peer reviews and mortality reviews, the focus remains on conducting open discussion within a nonpunitive environment driven toward prevention. When we engage in the careful work of reviewing safety incidents with an eye toward identifying all relevant factors, we transform healthcare organizations to have robust prevention programs—ones in which sharing observations through reporting is honored as a means of protecting patients and employees and increasing the well-being of all involved in the care process.

---

115 "Toolkit for Using the AHRQ Quality Indicators: How to Improve Hospital Quality and Safety, Selected Best Practices and Suggestions for Improvement," AHRQ, accessed August 23, 2022, https://www.ahrq.gov/patient-safety/settings/hospital/resource/qitool/index.html.

CHAPTER 7

Checklists for Prevention

*Checklists are basic tools of quality and productivity in
every field combining high risk and complexity.*

—Atul Gawande, The Checklist Manifesto: How to Get Things Right

When the COVID-19 outbreak rapidly spread across the country, the staff in Reese's skilled nursing facility had to adjust to a new set of processes and protocols to avoid the spread of infection among patients and employees. Because they already had a patient safety and incident reporting software in place for submitting information and managing events, they were able to build new intake forms to collect and track new data points, such as employee assessments, alternate work arrangements, health status reporting, environmental surveillance, infection control measures, and testing and vaccination status. Quickly innovating and deploying new tools enabled them to get ahead of the curve—to be proactive, rather than merely reactive, in their approach to the imminent threat of infection. "I was in contact with people in my same position at other skilled nursing facilities," Reese observed, "and I would listen to their harrowing stories about being unable to monitor employee and patient exposure to infection or push out surveys to assess resident and staff health status. But with the tools we deployed using our existing patient safety software, we were informed and able to adapt quickly. To date, we have conducted over seventy thousand employee health checks prior to employees reporting for their shifts and prevented employees who were infected or exposed to COVID-19 from furthering the spread."

Pandemic Tools

Employee Assessment

Check-in and report health status and COVID-19 exposures

Alternate Work Arrangements

Monitor workforce readiness and manage alternate work arrangement requests

Health Status Reporting

For employees returning to work, track and manage their health, safety, and exposure

Isolation Precautions

Observation of infection control compliance in patient isolation rooms

Infection Control

Monitor hand hygiene adherence and daily temperature checks to manage and remediate risks

Testing and Vaccination Status

Track and manage employees' COVID-19 test results, antibody screening, and vaccination status

Among three important strategies—preventing, recognizing, and mitigating harm—implementing actions to *prevent* harm has the greatest potential effect.[116] An organization that evolves into a *proactive* system of prevention is characterized by a high volume of near-miss reporting, improved communication and education, and

116 Molla Sloane Donaldson, An Overview of To Err Is Human: Re-Emphasizing the Message of Patient Safety, chap. 3 (Rockville, MD: Agency for Healthcare Research and Quality, 2008), https://www.ncbi.nlm.nih.gov/books/NBK2673/.

the implementation of systems and processes to get ahead of potential areas of risk before they become full-fledged problems. A strong support structure for prevention involves the careful utilization of a patient and employee rounding technology as well as automated checklists for surveying and proactively monitoring environments where care is delivered.

An organization that evolves into a *proactive* system of prevention is characterized by a high volume of near-miss reporting, improved communication and education, and the implementation of systems and processes to get ahead of potential areas of risk.

Recall that the key elements of a just culture include the following:

- Emphasis on *reporting* in an environment that focuses on learning from near misses and incidents and identifies all contributing factors of an event—not solely human factors. (We reviewed structures for successful reporting processes in chapters 3 and 4.)
- Organizational commitment to *analyze* events for continuous system and process improvements. (We reviewed processes for the follow-up and analysis of events and near misses in chapters 5 and 6.)
- Designing healthcare delivery processes to *prevent* failures and harm to patients and employees. (This is our focus here in chapter 7.)[117]

---

117 K. W. Kizer, "Large System Change and a Culture of Safety," in Enhancing Patient Safety and Reducing Errors in Health Care (Chicago, IL: National Patient Safety Foundation, 1999).

Why Checklists?

A checklist is defined as a list of action items arranged in a systematic manner that allows the user to consistently perform each action and record the completion of the individual items.[118] Safety checklists detail items that care teams should ask about or observe on a regular basis to ensure that standards are being met.[119] The specific items on a safety checklist will vary by organization and department, but all checklists should have a clear and organized format to make them simple for team members to follow.

Checklists are tools for improving and ensuring patient safety in various clinical settings by strengthening compliance with guidelines and by reducing incidents. A study by Johns Hopkins Hospital found that the introduction of a five-step safety checklist reduced the rate of bloodstream infections caused by intravenous lines by 67 percent, while on average, intensive care units cut their infection rates from nearly 3 percent of patients treated to 0 percent. During the eighteen months of the study, an estimated fifteen hundred lives were saved due to the implementation of safety checklists.[120]

Technology-enabled checklists can ensure that steps are followed each time so that healthcare workers can avoid reliance on memory and/or vigilance. Checklists reduce the risk of behavioral "slips" that might occur as a result of a care team's fatigue, distraction, or lapses in concentration. In addition to supporting those who are highly skilled yet are working in fast-paced, high-volume environments, standard-

---

118   B. M. Hales and P. J. Pronovost, "The Checklist: A Tool for Error Management and Performance Improvement," Journal of Critical Care 21 (2006): 213–235.

119   Øyvind Thomassen, "Implementation of Checklists in Health Care: Learning from High-Reliability Organisations," Scandinavian Journal of Trauma, Resuscitation and Emergency Medicine 19, no. 53 (2011), https://www.ncbi.nlm.nih.gov/pmc/articles/PMC3205016/.

120   Humphreys, G. (2008, July). Bulletin of the World Health Organization.

ized checklists ensure that those who are in training or of varying skill levels can follow approved protocols.

There have been multiple publications citing examples of the effective use of checklists in healthcare.[121] Early research includes a 2003 study utilizing a checklist to help a healthcare team better understand daily patient care goals in the surgical intensive care unit at Johns Hopkins Hospital. Over an eight-week period using a daily goals checklist, there was demonstrated improvement in the care team's understanding of the patient's care plan—from 10 percent to 95 percent. As a result of improved understanding of the plan of care, patient length of stay was reduced by 50 percent, from 2.2 days to 1.1 days.[122]

Checklists may also be utilized to ensure that performance improvement measures are occurring with regular frequency. For example, catheter-associated urinary tract infections (CAUTI) are some of the most common healthcare-acquired infections (HAI). Research has shown that approximately 50 percent of these infections are preventable.[123] An analysis by researchers at the College of Medicine at Penn State University revealed that costs associated with CAUTI range from $876 to $10,197, depending on the patient's acuity and resources available in the specific hospital setting where they occur.[124] There are evidence-based components of the CAUTI bundle that lend themselves well to

---

121   Included among these are: C. S. Hollenbeak and A. L. Schilling, "The Attributable Cost of Catheter-Associated Urinary Tract Infections in the United States: A Systematic Review," American Journal of Infection Control 46, no. 7 (2018): 751–757, www.sciencedirect.com/science/article/pii/S0196655318300361 and S. Saint et al., "A Program to Prevent Catheter-Associated Urinary Tract Infection in Acute Care," New England Journal of Medicine 374 (2016): 2111–2119, www.nejm.org/doi/full/10.1056/NEJMoa1504906#t=articleResults.

122   P. Pronovost et al., "Improving Communication in the ICU Using Daily Goals."

123   R. M. Klevens, et al., "Estimating Healthcare Associated Infection and Death in US Hospitals," Public Health Report 122, no. 2 (2007): 160–166.

124   C. S. Hollenbeak and A. L. Schilling, "The Attributable Cost."

an automated checklist.[125] In a recent study that reviewed CAUTI data from 926 units (59.7 percent were non-ICUs, and 40.3 percent were ICUs) in 603 hospitals across 32 states, the results showed a decrease in CAUTI and overall catheter use in non-ICU settings when AHRQ checklists and other tools were utilized.[126]

Although it is typical for healthcare practitioners to create their own checklists for self-use, standardized and institutionalized checklists have the benefit of having been tested for validity and reliability. By their very design, they "provide unambiguous guidance on what, when, how, and who should do a particular intervention."[127]

With standardized checklists, healthcare organizations can do the following:

- **Promote more effective rounding.** Standardized, automated checklists promote rounding that is focused and methodical and can be deployed with consistency.
- **Improve quality monitoring.** Checklists allow employees to share data, measure outcomes, and track clinical performance across care teams, departments, and the organization overall. With automated checklists, managers can track when checklists are deployed and query data points from fields within the checklists to identify areas of potential risk.
- **Minimize environment of care risks.** Checklists help minimize or eliminate risks by monitoring the patient environment for safety and satisfaction of basic requirements.

---

125 M. Hanchett, "Preventing CAUTI: A Patient-Centered Approach," Prevention Strategist (Autumn 2012): 43–49.

126 S. Saint et al., "A Program to Prevent Catheter-Associated Urinary Tract Infection."

127 B. D. Winters et al., "Clinical Review: Checklist—Translating Evidence into Practice," Critical Care 13, no. 210 (2009), http://ccforum.com/content/13/6/210.

- **Engage in benchmarking.** Automated checklists enable the comparison of existing processes to best practices, offering a powerful way to gain insights that can lead to improved performance.

An automated checklist has these benefits: it is *available* at all times; it has the ability to be *revised easily*, according to latest evidence and best practices; it is *visible* to multiple members of a healthcare team; it *decreases the risk* of mistaken calculations; and it gives leadership the opportunity to *monitor* progress and compliance. Yet another distinct advantage of the standardization of checklists is the use of common language and terminology. Finally, automated checklists reduce the risk of miscommunication and misinterpretation, ensuring that "the same knowledge is available to doctors, nurses, and patients."[128]

Types of Checklists

There are multiple types of checklists that healthcare teams can use to improve outcomes:

- The **laundry list checklist** includes items, tasks, or criteria grouped into related categories in no particular order. A list of medical equipment used in a given procedure is an example of the laundry list checklist.
- The **sequential checklist** consists of items that are to be performed in a given order to obtain a valid outcome. An example is a checklist that ensures the relevant flow of actions takes place when performing a particular clinical procedure.

---

128   Ibid

- The **iterative checklist** includes items or tasks that require repeated passes or review to obtain valid results. An example is an hourly rounding checklist to prevent falls.
- The **diagnostic checklist** contains items in a flowchart for drawing broad conclusions. Clinical algorithms are examples of diagnostic checklists.
- The **criteria of merit checklist** is used to evaluate the flow of information in order to ensure the objectivity and reliability of conclusions drawn. An example is the post-fall root cause analysis checklist.[129]

Every item on a safety checklist should be clearly defined and have a specific associated action if the item is not met. For instance, if the checklist question "Are all hallways free of clutter?" is answered "No," then there should be a process in place to notify the maintenance team to clear the hallway as well as a process to confirm whether the hallway has been satisfactorily cleared. Software can aid in triggering and tracking these details by automatically notifying facilities of a cleanup after a "No" answer trigger. It can also be used to facilitate team communications regarding checklist items, to set reminders or proactively launch checklists, to guide users through the checklist completion process, and to gather and analyze data at varied levels of the organization.

Utilization of Checklists

Organizations that have successfully implemented rounding checklists experience decreases in incidents and high levels of patient and staff

---

129   B. Hales et al., "Development of Medical Checklists for Improved Quality of Patient Care," International Journal of Quality in Health Care 20 (December 2008): 22–30.

satisfaction.[130] Along with improving patient safety, rounding check-lists create a greater sense of confidence that processes are completed accurately and thoroughly.[131] One study found that hourly rounding in fourteen hospitals yielded the following improvements:

- A 12 percent increase in patient satisfaction scores.
- A 52 percent reduction in patient falls.
- A 37 percent reduction in light use.
- A 14 percent decline in skin breakdowns.
- One hospital measured a 20 percent reduction in the distance walked each day by the nursing staff.[132]

Rounding checklists promote an environment of safety by

- enforcing a safe environment,
- ensuring that all equipment is checked,
- eliminating and/or reducing behaviors and processes that could result in harm,
- providing a focus on patient assistance,
- identifying issues and deficiencies before they develop into safety events,
- demonstrating a commitment to change, and
- reducing patient falls, infections, and pressure ulcers.[133]

---

130   Donna Fabry, "Hourly Rounding: Perspectives and Perceptions of the Frontline Nursing Staff," Journal of Nursing Management 23, no. 2 (March 2015): 200–210, https://onlinelibrary.wiley.com/doi/abs/10.1111/jonm.12114.

131   "Checklists to Improve Patient Safety," Hospitals in Pursuit of Excellence, June 2013, http://www.hpoe.org/Reports-HPOE/CkLists_PatientSafety.pdf.

132   Performance Health Partners. (n.d.). 4 steps to purposeful patient rounding. Performance Health Partners Healthcare Technology I Incident Reporting. Retrieved August 24, 2022, from https://www.performancehealthus.com/blog/4-steps-to-purposeful-patient-rounding

133   5 Benefits to Implementing a Rounding Solution. https://sentact.com/. (n.d.). Retrieved August 24, 2022, from chrome-extension://efaidnbmnnnibpcajpcglclefindmkaj/https://sentact.com/wp-content/uploads/2020/06/5BenefitsRoundingSolution.pdf.

Healthcare organizations that implement rounding checklists will inevitably discover areas for improvement. A rounding tool helps organizations track data over time to improve processes in the future.[134]

Checklists & Clinical Rounding Tools

Use Case 1: Infection Prevention

Each year, the global community becomes more aware of how important it is to prevent, detect, and respond to infectious diseases. New pathogens are emerging every day and evolving to resist treatments. This is in addition to the frequent threat of preventable harm that patients and employees already face in daily healthcare delivery.

Between the harmful effects of pandemics and the high prevalence of preventable healthcare-acquired infections (HAIs), organizations are reevaluating how infection prevention and control tie into patient safety. The COVID-19 crisis has highlighted the demand for organizations to adopt a multidisciplinary approach in which patients and staff collaborate to strengthen emergency response and prevent disease.[135]

134   5 Benefits to Implementing a Rounding Solution. https://sentact.com/. (n.d.). Retrieved August 24, 2022, from chrome-extension://efaidnbmnnnibpcajpcglclefindmkaj/https://sentact.com/wp-content/uploads/2020/06/5BenefitsRoundingSolution.pdf

135   "HAI Data," Centers for Disease Control and Prevention, updated October 5, 2018, https://www.cdc.gov/hai/data/index.html.

According to the Centers for Disease Control and Prevention, HAIs are contracted by an estimated 1.7 million patients annually and are responsible for ninety-nine thousand deaths each year in the United States alone.[136] All patients are at risk of contracting an HAI while being treated for another medical condition.[137] With the rise of healthcare-associated infections in recent years, it is critical that organizations take a proactive approach toward infection control and prevention to provide the safest possible environment for both patients and staff.

> Each year, the global community becomes more aware of how important it is to prevent, detect, and respond to infectious diseases.

The first step toward preventing infection is to establish processes for evaluating infection control measures during daily routines.

An infection prevention rounding checklist might ask the following questions:

- Is PPE transported in enclosed carts or containers?
- Are the carts or containers free from damage?
- Is clean attire stored in an employee locker?
- Are scrubs removed before employees leave the healthcare organization?
- Are hand hygiene protocols observed?

Pittet et al. reported decreased HAI infection rates, from 16.9 percent to 9.9 percent, over a four-year period and reduced MRSA

---

136 Centers for Disease Control and Prevention. (2019, November 6). Patient safety: What you can do to be a safe patient. Centers for Disease Control and Prevention. Retrieved August 24, 2022, from https://www.cdc.gov/HAI/patientSafety/patient-safety.html

137 "HAI Data," Centers for Disease Control and Prevention.

acquisition and infection rates with improved hand hygiene and alcohol-based rub use. Doebbeling et al. reported reducing HAIs by 28 percent through the introduction of new handwashing agents. Other studies have shown the impact of improved hand hygiene on decreased infection and transmission.[138]

If we take protocols and processes for hand hygiene as an example of the way an infection prevention checklist might be developed, an organization will begin by identifying existing factors influencing noncompliance with hand hygiene protocols. Centers for Disease Control and Prevention research shows that on average, healthcare personnel clean their hands fewer than half of the times they should.[139] Environmental factors influencing noncompliance with hand hygiene protocol vary between organizations and can include lack of soap at handwashing stations or lack of training around hand hygiene protocol, such as using soap, washing all surfaces of one's hands for fifteen to twenty seconds, thoroughly drying one's hands, and turning the faucet off with a towel to avoid touching the dirty surface.[140]

Healthcare workers may wash their hands less when their workloads become more intense as well as toward the ends of their shifts, when they're more likely to be mentally and physically drained.[141] Others may require specific training on safety protocols; for instance, many believe that wearing gloves eliminates the need for

138 Performance Health Partners. (n.d.). 4 steps to purposeful patient rounding. Performance Health Partners Healthcare Technology I Incident Reporting. Retrieved August 24, 2022, from https://www.performancehealthus.com/blog/4-steps-to-purposeful-patient-rounding

139 "Clean Hands Count for Safe Healthcare," Centers for Disease Control and Prevention, updated February 25, 2020, https://www.cdc.gov/patientsafety/features/clean-hands-count.html.

140 Alisha Hrustic, "Study: 78% of Health-Care Workers Don't Properly Wash Their Hands," Men's Health, July 15, 2016, https://www.menshealth.com/health/a19524980/healthcare-workers-dont-wash-their-hands/.

141 Hengchen Dai et al., "The Impact of Time at Work and Time Off from Work on Rule Compliance: The Case of Hand Hygiene in Health Care," Journal of Applied Psychology 100, no. 3 (2015): 846–862, https://www.apa.org/pubs/journals/releases/apl-a0038067.pdf.

hand hygiene.[142] Additionally, under-resourced facilities may lack sufficient numbers of sinks or easily accessible soap and alcohol-based hand-rub solution to perform effective hand hygiene.[143]

It is important for healthcare organizations to identify the factors that may be preventing compliance to establish a hand hygiene process. Efforts might include ensuring that products are stored and dispensed according to manufacturers' instructions, so as not to become weakened or contaminated,[144] and well-placed reminders to employees and staff to keep in mind the "four moments of hand hygiene" for determining when to cleanse hands: (1) before contact with a patient, (2) before performing an antiseptic procedure, (3) after exposure to bodily fluids, and (4) after contact with a patient.[145]

> EOC rounding has become an increasingly useful tool for improving patient and staff engagement in safety promotion.

Use Case 2: Environment of Care (EOC) Rounding

As the healthcare industry has evolved to focus more on patient-centered care, Environment of Care (EOC) rounding has become an increasingly useful tool for improving patient and staff engagement in safety promotion. According to the Joint Commission, "protecting patients from harm involves more than safe treatments and proce-

---

142   "Clean Hands Count for Safe Healthcare," Centers for Disease Control and Prevention.

143   "Clean Hands Count for Safe Healthcare," Centers for Disease Control and Prevention.

144   "Hand Hygiene," Centers for Disease Control and Prevention, updated March 1, 2016, https://www.cdc.gov/oralhealth/infectioncontrol/faqs/hand-hygiene.html.

145   Anjum Chagpar et al., "Challenges of Hand Hygiene in Healthcare: The Development of a Tool Kit to Create Supportive Processes and Environments," Healthcare Quarterly 13 (October 2010): 59–66, https://www.longwoods.com/content/21968/healthcare-quarterly/challenges-of-hand-hygiene-in-healthcare-the-development-of-a-tool-kit-to-create-supportive-process.

dures. We must also consider where patients receive care and minimize risks associated with the physical environment."[146] EOC rounds play a critical role in ensuring the safety of patients and staff and optimizing the overall operations of a healthcare facility.

Every action item on an EOC rounding checklist should be clearly defined and have a specific person assigned to the task to ensure that it is properly completed. An EOC rounding checklist might ask questions such as these:

- Does the room need to be rearranged (with the patient's permission) to clear paths?
- Are all examination tables adjusted into locked position?
- Has the room been arranged so that items are within the patient's reach (e.g., are walking aids within safe reach)?
- Are there any high, broken, or missing thresholds that need to be replaced?
- Are there any burned out or flickering light bulbs or call lights that need to be replaced?
- Are there any exposed cords hanging in the room?
- Have any clean glove boxes been placed on top of used sharps containers?
- Are all hallways clear of equipment?
- Are emergency exits clear of obstructions?
- Are wet-floor signs used and removed in a timely manner?

---

146 "The Physical Environment," The Joint Commission, accessed August 23, 2022, https://www.jointcommission.org/en/resources/patient-safety-topics/the-physical-environment/.

Use Case 3: Safety Huddles

Safety huddles are defined as routine, brief meetings usually at the beginning of the workday, comprised of staff from varying disciplines.[147] The meeting is a time for care teams to discuss patient safety events, relay information about areas of safety concern (e.g., short staffing, equipment, inventory), and establish safety goals.[148] Safety huddles allow teams to communicate about targeted concerns, share information, and identify improvements that can be made to efforts across the organization. Huddles have been shown to improve patient safety in a variety of areas, such as falls, wrong-site surgery, and near misses.[149]

A study of an acute-care hospital showed that when four nursing units adopted regular safety huddles, there was a significant reduction in falls, from 12.4 to just 5 falls per week.[150] The study also showed improvements in 23 out of 27 parameters of the organization's culture survey.[151] These brief meetings have been shown to improve the efficiency of information sharing, enhance a sense of accountability and empowerment of staff, and increase the sense of community across different departments and units.[152]

Huddle leaders prepare any necessary updates and information for the meeting ahead of time and facilitate the meeting according

147 "Safety Huddles: Guide to Safety Huddles," Patient Safety, Washington State Hospital Association, March 4, 2015, http://www.wsha.org/wp-content/uploads/Worker-Safety_SafetyHuddleTool-kit_3_27_15.pdf.

148 Alison Cracknell et al., "Huddle Up for Safer Healthcare: How Frontline Teams Can Work Together to Improve Patient Safety," Future Hospital Journal 3, no. 2 (June 1, 2016): s31, https://www.ncbi.nlm.nih.gov/pmc/articles/PMC6465903/.

149 Ulfat Shaikh, "Improving Patient Safety and Team Communication through Daily Huddles," Patient Safety Network, January 29, 2020, https://psnet.ahrq.gov/primer/improving-patient-safety-and-team-communication-through-daily-huddles.

150 Alison Cracknell et al., "Huddle Up for Safer Healthcare."

151 Alison Cracknell et al., "Huddle Up for Safer Healthcare."

152 Linda M. Goldenhar et al., "Huddling for High Reliability and Situation Awareness," BMJ Quality and Safety 22 (2013): 899–906, https://qualitysafety.bmj.com/content/22/11/899.

to an agenda in the form of a checklist that maximizes the use of time. Consistency improves attendance—a key component to making safety huddles successful—and allows everyone to come prepared, contribute, and collaborate toward identifying useful takeaways.[153] An example safety huddle checklist agenda is this:

- Announcements
- Successes with patient safety yesterday
- Concerns with patient safety yesterday
- Safety risks for today's patients
- Performance on patient safety measures
- Updates on organization-wide patient safety initiatives[154]

Use Case 4: Individual Risk Assessments

An example of an *individual risk assessment* is the identification and management of each patient's underlying fall-risk factors while proactively addressing the underlying causes that may lead to a fall and optimizing the physical environment to avoid creating fall hazards.[155] A fall prevention rounding checklist guides the healthcare team in interactions with patients that *educate* them about fall prevention practices, *assist* them with mobility, and *partner* with them in a commitment to work together.

Meade et al. were among the first to publish positive outcomes of a multifaceted fall prevention program that included hourly rounding on patients at high risk. Results showed a reduction of falls from twenty-five during the four-week period prior to starting the program

---

153   Alison Cracknell et al., "Huddle Up for Safer Healthcare."

154   Ulfat Shaikh, "Improving Patient Safety and Team Communication."

155   The Joint Commission, Physician Leader Monthly, March 2018, https://www.jointcommission.org/assets /1/18/Physician_Leader_Monthly_March_2018.pdf.

to twelve during the four-week intervention period.[156] Other health-care facilities have reported improvements ranging from a 28 percent reduction to a 33 percent reduction in fall rates after implementing fall prevention programs.[157]

Use Case 5: Patient Experience

Whenever possible, patients and their families or other caregivers should be invited to participate in the care and safety process. Ensuring patient and family engagement helps clinicians obtain accurate information about details like each patient's medications, allergies, and current health status. Safety improves when patients and their families all know the patients' conditions, treatments, and any technologies that are used in their care.

In 2007, the Joint Commission mandated that healthcare organizations "encourage patients' active involvement in their own care as a patient safety strategy," catalyzing research into how patients may inadvertently hasten safety events as well as how they may partner with providers to prevent them.[158] Research has shown the achievement of sustainable improvements in patient outcomes when organizations' patient safety culture is pervasive in all interactions with patients and their families.[159] Patients' involvement in their own care has, in more recent years, been recognized as a key component in the advancement of patient safety.

156 C. M. Meade et al., "Effects of Nursing Rounds on Patients' Call Light Use, Satisfaction and Safety," American Journal of Nursing 106, no. 9 (2006): 58–70.

157 C. M. Walsh et al., "Temporal Trends in Fall Rates with the Implementation of a Multifaceted Fall Prevention Program: Persistence Pays Off," The Joint Commission Journal on Quality and Patient Safety 44, no. 75 (2018), https://www.jointcommissionjournal.com/article/S1553-7250(17)30350-1/pdf.

158 "11 Tenets of a Safety Culture," The Joint Commission.

159 K. W. Kizer, "Large System Change and a Culture of Safety."

Efforts to engage patients in safety initiatives have focused on three areas:

- Enlisting patients in detecting incidents
- Empowering patients to ensure their safe care
- Emphasizing patient involvement as a means of improving safety[160]

Making incident reporting tools accessible to patients and their families closes the gap between patient safety and patient experience efforts. When employees, patients, and their caregivers are engaged in detecting safety challenges and reporting their observations, an organization's opportunities for preventing harm increase.

Practicing patient-centered care encourages active collaboration and shared decision making between patients, families, and providers to provide a more comprehensive, high-quality care experience. It is beneficial not only for patients but also for health systems, as it encourages productivity among clinicians, improved resource allocation, and reduced expenses. This collaborative approach to care also minimizes patient stress.

A safety-oriented patient engagement checklist might look like this:

160   "Patient Engagement and Safety," Patient Safety Network.

Patient Experience Form

Identify

Leader Name

_____

Patient Name

_____

Room Number

_____

Greetings

- [ ] Knock on door, request permission to enter.
- [ ] Greet patient by name.
- [ ] Acknowledge family/visitors in room.
- [ ] Use approachable body language (e.g. maintain eye contact, smile).
- [ ] Introduce self, skill set, and relevant certifications.
- [ ] Explain purpose of visit (e.g. "Our goal is to ensure your visit with us exceeds your expectations. We'd like to better understand how we can do that.").

Evaluate Employee Behavior

- [ ] Ask open-ended questions to solicit feedback around staff behavior (e.g. "How well is our team explaining the procedures you're scheduled for?" "How would you describe communication with your care team?").

Employee Recognition

☐ Ask patients which employees they've engaged with deserve to be recognized and rewarded for a job well done.

Closing Statement

☐ Ask, "Is there anything I can do to improve your experience with us?"

☐ Thank the patient for their feedback.

Communication with Employees

☐ Recognize and reward employees demonstrating exceptional behavior and service.

☐ Provide additional training to employees whose behavior is unsatisfactory.

Service Recovery

☐ Apologize when the patient's expectations are not met by the organization (e.g. "I'm sorry you had that experience.").

☐ Ask questions to better understand patient's expectations and act to resolve the issue (e.g. "What can I do to address your concerns?").

☐ Follow up to confirm that the patient's concerns were addressed/resolved.

Use Case 6: Employee Experience

Employee rounding has been found to be the single most effective tool for making employees feel heard and appreciated.[161] When healthcare organizations increase engagement by conducting executive rounds of caregiver teams, it helps leadership understand concerns and take appropriate action to improve employee safety and satisfaction.[162] In addition to addressing concerns and identifying areas of improvement, employee rounding goes a long way toward promoting effective communication and transparency among care teams.

It is important that each department provides adequate equipment and training on safety protocols so that employees understand their responsibilities. Staff members should be regularly updated on related policy changes, and organizations should consider establishing a rapid response safety team or a set of employees specifically assigned to addressing harmful safety incidents.[163] Just as every employee must understand their specific roles and responsibilities in upholding organizational safety, so, too, may organizations need to implement new procedures and workflows to ensure that adequate processes are in place for prioritizing safety and avoiding employee burnout.

A simple employee safety rounding checklist might ask the following questions:

- What's working well?
- Do you have the resources you need to perform your job?

161   5 Benefits to Implementing a Rounding Solution. https://sentact.com/. (n.d.). Retrieved August 24, 2022, from chrome-extension://efaidnbmnnnibpcajpcglclefindmkaj/https://sentact.com/wp-content/uploads/2020/06/5BenefitsRoundingSolution.pdf.

162   5 Benefits to Implementing a Rounding Solution. https://sentact.com/. (n.d.). Retrieved August 24, 2022, from chrome-extension://efaidnbmnnnibpcajpcglclefindmkaj/https://sentact.com/wp-content/uploads/2020/06/5BenefitsRoundingSolution.pdf.

163   "7 Tips for Ensuring Patient Safety in Health Care Settings," Regis College, November 2, 2021, https://online.regiscollege.edu/blog/7-tips-ensuring-patient-safety-healthcare-settings/.

- What's not working well that makes it difficult to do your job?
- What improvement suggestions do you have?
- Who are the people that we should be highlighting for excellent work?[164]

A more involved checklist tool might look something like the following:

164 "The Framework for High Reliability Healthcare," Safe and Reliable Healthcare, accessed August 23, 2022, https://www.safeandreliablecare.com/the-framework-for-high-reliability-healthcare.

Employee Engagement Form

Employee Name

_____

Date

_____ 📅

Personal Life

Ask question to convey concern for employee's wellbeing outside of work (e.g. "What have you been growing in your garden lately?" "Have you been on any hikes recently?"). Use Employee Preference Cards to identify outside interests, hobbies, etc.

Employee reponse:

_____

Action items:

_____

Wins

General — "What has been working well for you these days?"

Employee reponse:

_____

Action items:

_____

Targeted — "What is working well with _____ ?"

Employee reponse:

_____

Action items:

_____

Recognition

General — "Is there a staff member, department, or physician that I should recognize for doing an exceptional job?"

Employee reponse:

_____

Action items:

_____

Targeted — "Who was especially helpful with _____ ?"

Employee reponse:

_____

Action items:

_____

Processes

General — "What hospital systems are not working well for you? What are your ideas to fix them?"

Employee reponse:

Action items:

Targeted — "What with _____ needs improvement? How can we make positive change?"

Employee reponse:

Action items:

Needs

General — "Do you have the tools and equipment you need to do your job today?"

Employee reponse:

Action items:

Targeted — "What tools and equipment are needed to improve the _____ process further?"

Employee reponse:

Action items:

Expectations

General — "Do you know what is expected of you at work?"

Employee reponse:

Action items:

Closing Statement

"Is there anything I can do before I leave?

Employee reponse:

"Do you have any questions for me?"

Employee reponse:

Thank the employee for their time and feedback.

Checking In

Checklists and other rounding tools allow us regularly to *check in* with one another, to open lines of communication, and to create ongoing dialogue among team members and in relation to facility leadership. The use of checklists is not simply a direct means of preventing harm by ensuring that existing standards are met; it is also a means of contributing to employees' and patients' physical and emotional safety and sense of being heard within the care environment.

PART III

CHAPTER 8

Patient Safety as a Value-Based Care Initiative

Why we're doing [value-based care models] is we are going to get better outcomes and lower costs, but it's also about building a better health system for everyone.

—Mark McCellan, MD, PhD, director and professor of business
policy, Margolis Center for Health Policy, Duke University

P ayment models used by healthcare organizations have evolved over time. One of the most significant healthcare paradigm shifts in the past decade has been the introduction of a new reimbursement model known as value-based care. Healthcare reimbursement describes the payment that a healthcare provider receives for providing patients with medical services. In a value-based system, a portion or all of provider payments are based on patient and/or value-based care network outcomes. Where the traditional fee-for-service model compensated organizations on the *quantity* of care provided, the value-based care model incentivizes organizations to provide the highest *quality* of care.[165]

This chapter emphasizes patient safety as a pillar of value-based care. The reporting-centric and outcomes-focused aspects of patient safety programs work in tandem with the quality-centric elements of value-based care.

Value-based care models emphasize an integrated team approach and care coordination, including care delivery models, such as medical homes, accountable care organizations, bundled payments, capitation, and shared savings and risk. Rather than focus on the structure of value-based care networks, in this chapter we will focus on the ways in which patient safety is critical to achieving the intended quality outcomes of value-based care, including cost reduction, increased patient engagement and satisfaction, effective clinical care, reduction in medical errors, and overall improvement in population health.

Patient safety focuses on the avoidance of incidents and absence of harm. *Quality* is providing efficient, effective, purposeful care that is focused on improving a patient's health outcomes. If safety measures make it less likely that harm will occur, quality measures raise the ceiling so that the overall experience and care outcome is a better one. A focus on value, understood as a concern with both quality and safety, requires optimizing the use of available resources for the sake of patient and population outcomes.[166] When we bring efforts in value-based care into conjunction with patient safety and quality care initiatives, we begin to see how patient and employee involvement in care coordination stands alongside other critical components we've

---

165 "Value-Based Care," Cleveland Clinic, updated October 19, 2020, https://my.clevelandclinic.org/health/articles/15938-value-based-care.

166 "Quality of Care," Center for Medicare Advocacy, accessed August 23, 2022, https://medicareadvocacy.org/medicare-info/quality-of-care/.

emphasized in previous chapters: the reporting of safety events, an emphasis on learning from incidents and near misses, and the implementation of prevention tools. Integrating patient safety measures into value-based healthcare has the potential to improve patient experiences and safety and clinical outcomes while also aiding the optimal allocation of finite resources in our organizations.

The Evolution of Value-Based Reimbursement

If we focus on the past fifty years of healthcare reforms, a few efforts stand out as part of the press toward increased quality of care. The Health Maintenance Organization (HMO) Act of 1973, enacted during the Nixon administration, was intended to contain costs and improve healthcare quality for populations that were previously underserved. By the time the act took effect, fee-for-service medicine had led to healthcare inflation because the focus was on treating patients when they were sick. Providers were not compensated for keeping patients well, and as a result, the HMO era did not lead to significant quality for the price of healthcare.

Following the passage of the Patient Protection and Affordable Care Act (ACA) in 2010, during the Obama administration, reimbursements became tied to patient satisfaction and the quality—rather than the quantity—of care provided.[167] The Affordable Care Act established the Hospital Value-Based Purchasing Program, a CMS initiative that "rewards acute-care hospitals with incentive payments for the quality of care provided."[168]

---

167 Hospital value-based purchasing. CMS. (n.d.). Retrieved August 24, 2022, from https://www.cms. gov/Medicare/Quality-Initiatives-Patient-Assessment-Instruments/Value-Based-Programs/HVBP/ Hospital-Value-Based-Purchasing

168 "Hospital Value-Based Purchasing," Centers for Medicare & Medicaid Services.

With the shift toward value-based purchasing, CMS turned to reimbursing hospitals based on

- the quality of care provided to patients,
- how closely best clinical practices are followed, and
- how well hospitals enhance patients' experiences of care during hospital stays.[169]

Upon its passage, it was estimated that the ACA would provide coverage for over 94 percent of Americans.[170] Even though there was greater coverage than had existed prior, the ACA continues to labor to achieve its goal of providing more affordable health insurance to almost every American.[171] Healthcare insurance premiums continue to be costly and unaffordable for many of those whom the introduction of the ACA was intended to help.

In 2015, the secretary of Health and Human Services and CMS directed still another shift toward a value-based payment program, the Pay for Performance (P4P) model, which "ties reimbursement to metric-driven outcomes, proven best practices, and patient satisfaction, thus aligning payment with value and quality."[172] Hospitals are not the only organizations impacted by P4P. Other value-based payment programs include the End-Stage Renal Disease Quality Initiative Program, the Skilled Nursing Facility Value-Based Program, the Home Health Value-Based Program, and the Value Modifier or Value-Based Modifier Program.

---

169   "Hospital Value-Based Purchasing," Centers for Medicare & Medicaid Services.

170   Lori Robertson, "Not Everybody Is Covered under ACA," FactCheck.org, April 2, 2014, https://www.factcheck.org/2014/04/not-everybody-is-covered-under-aca/.

171   D. Parker, Pay for Performance vs. Fee for Service: Why You Should Care How Your Doctor Gets Paid, The Benefits Guide, Anthem, July 13, 2015.

172   "What Is Pay for Performance in Healthcare?," Innovation in Care Delivery, NEJM Catalyst, updated March 1, 2018, https://catalyst.nejm.org/pay-for-performance-in-healthcare/.

P4P and the Medicare Access and the Children's Health Insurance Program (CHIP) Reauthorization Act (also issued in 2015) were both enacted to improve payments to physicians and other clinicians while rewarding value and outcomes via a Quality Payment Program. Eligible clinicians participate either as individuals or groups and in one of two tracks: (a) a Merit-Based Incentive Payment System (MIPS), or (b) Advanced Alternative Payment Models (Advanced APMs).

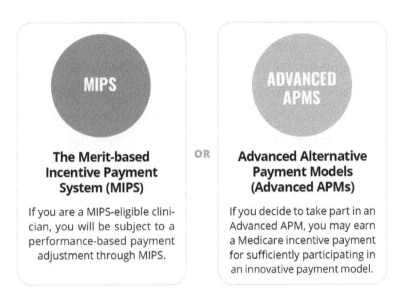

The Merit-based Incentive Payment System (MIPS)

OR

Advanced Alternative Payment Models (Advanced APMs)

If you are a MIPS-eligible clinician, you will be subject to a performance-based payment adjustment through MIPS.

If you decide to take part in an Advanced APM, you may earn a Medicare incentive payment for sufficiently participating in an innovative payment model.

Clinicians are expected to actively measure and report their quality efforts. There are more than 250 quality measures in MIPS, and clinicians may report on "at least six quality measures, including at least one outcome measure or a high priority measure."[173]

Those 250 MIPS quality measures fall into six domains:

- Patient safety
- Person and caregiver-centered experience and outcomes

---

173 "ASC Quality Reporting," Centers for Medicare & Medicaid Services, accessed October 24, 2019, https://www.cms.gov/Medicare/Quality-Initiatives-Patient-Assessment-Instruments/ASC-Quality-Reporting/.

- Communication and care coordination
- Effective clinical care
- Community/population health
- Efficiency and cost reduction

Once all data is submitted, Medicare payments are adjusted for eligible clinicians based on their MIPS final score.[174, 175] For example, physician quality outcome scores as measured by MIPS are available to the public via the website Physician Compare approximately twelve months following a given reporting period.

The significance of these transformations is this: as healthcare costs and forms of reimbursement have evolved over time, so have the models of care used by healthcare organizations. With the movement toward value-based care, organizations are driven to achieve higher levels of patient safety, patient experience, care coordination, effective clinical care, and efficiency so that they can maximize reimbursement and maintain fiscal stability but also—and most importantly—improve community and population health. The most profound way in which the goal of value-based care dovetails with the goal of patient safety programs is that *it puts greater emphasis on making healthcare preventive.*

With this goal in mind, a framework of value in healthcare called "the value equation" has emerged:

$$\text{Value (V)} = \frac{\text{Quality (Q) + Service (S)}}{\text{Cost (\$)}}$$

174 "2019 Merit-Based Incentive Payment System (MIPS) Quality Performance Category Fact Sheet," Centers for Medicare & Medicaid Services, accessed October 24, 2019

175 "Fact Sheet: 2019 Merit-Based Incentive Payment Adjustments Based on 2017 MIPS Scores," Centers for Medicare & Medicaid Services, accessed October 24, 2019, from https://qpp-cm-prod-content.s3.amazonaws.com/uploads/70/2019%20MIPS%20Payment%20Adjustment%20Fact%20Sheet_2018%2011%2029.pdf.

where the value of the service is directly related to the quality of care and outcomes achieved, as opposed merely to the quantity of provider visits.[176]

Value-based care programs have expanded rapidly across the United States, with a sevenfold increase in the number of states implementing such initiatives in the five-year period between 2015 and 2019. According to a study by Change Healthcare, as of April 2019,

> The most profound way in which the goal of value-based care dovetails with the goal of patient safety programs is that *it puts greater emphasis on making healthcare preventive.*

- forty-eight states had implemented value-based care or payment programs,
- fifty percent of those programs are multi-payer in scope, and
- just four states had few to no value-based care initiatives underway.[177]

Efforts supporting value-based care and reimbursement only further emphasize the increasing importance for healthcare organizations to focus on improving patient safety and quality.

Areas of opportunity that have emerged from the movement toward value-based care include the following:

---

176 Sam Peirce, "The History of Value-Based Care," Elation Health, updated June 3, 2022, https://www.elationhealth.com/healthcare-innovation-policy-news-blog/history-value/.

177 Change Healthcare Research: 48 states now committed to value-based care and payment models. Business Wire. (2019, April 16). Retrieved August 24, 2022, from https://www.businesswire.com/news/home/20190416005597/en/Change-Healthcare-Research-48-States-Now-Committed-to-Value-Based-Care-and-Payment-Models

1. **Improved patient outcomes.** Patient outcomes are the cornerstones of high-quality, value-based care. There are often small changes that can be made to improve outcomes and savings. Managing a chronic disease or condition like cancer, diabetes, high blood pressure, COPD, or obesity can be costly and time consuming for patients. Value-based care models focus on helping patients recover from illnesses and injuries more quickly and prevent or delay the onset of chronic disease. The intended result is that patients face fewer doctors' visits, medical tests, and procedures and spend less money on prescription medication, as both near-term and long-term health improve.

2. **Engaged patients.** Patient involvement in their own care has, in recent years, been recognized as a key component in the advancement of patient safety. Earlier, we learned that efforts to engage patients in safety initiatives have focused on three areas: enlisting patients in detecting incidents, empowering patients to voice their concerns to ensure their safe care, and emphasizing patient involvement as a means of improving the culture of safety. One way in which healthcare organizations can actively engage patients is to implement a patient relations survey tool wherein patients can easily give feedback on the care provided them. To address patients' hesitation to speak candidly about care received, feedback can be directed through an electronic reporting or survey tool instead of being shared directly with

> Patient outcomes are the cornerstones of high-quality, value-based care. There are often small changes that can be made to improve outcomes and savings.

particular caregiving staff. A patient safety technology platform facilitates direct patient involvement but also fosters clearer and more transparent communication between leadership, providers, and their patients.[178]

3. **Actively engaged staff.** Driving active staff engagement has become a major strategy for increasing value by combatting employee burnout and turnover. Craig Deao, a consultant for Huron and faculty member at the American College of Healthcare Executives, estimated that the average cost of employee turnover in healthcare is almost $27 million per year.[179] Employee engagement programs have emerged as a key tool for improving those rates. Engaging employees requires active organizational leadership commitment to staff members' psychological and physical safety in the workplace. According to *Healthcare Finance News*, "a focus on employees' commitment and emotional investment in their work is a 'must-have' core competency for leaders in healthcare" helping to increase engagement across departments.[180]

4. **Decreased harm and decreased costs.** National health spending is projected to grow at an average rate of 5.5 percent per year in the nine-year period from 2019 to 2027 and to reach nearly $6.0 trillion by 2027.[181] Maximizing annual reimbursements by delivering quality care increases organizations' abilities to profit and grow their resources. By

---

178   "Patient Engagement and Safety," Patient Safety Network.

179   Beth Jones Sanborn, "Cure for Healthcare's High Employee Turnover Is Engagement, Expert Says," Healthcare Finance News, July 18, 2017, https://www.healthcarefinancenews.com/news/cure-healthcares-high-employee-turnover-engagement-expert-says.

180   Beth Jones Sanborn, "Cure for Healthcare's High Employee Turnover."

181   "National Health Expenditure Projections 2018–2027," Centers for Medicare & Medicaid Services, accessed August 23, 2022, https://www.cms.gov/Research-Statistics-Data-and-Systems/Statistics-Trends-and-Reports/NationalHealthExpendData/Downloads/ForecastSummary.pdf.

clearly centering patient safety, healthcare organizations can improve quality of care, lower the cost of care, and increase value-based care reimbursements.

The Impact of Patient Safety Programs on Patient Outcomes

Patient safety programs have meaningful impacts on making care safer through the prevention of HACs, conditions that a patient develops while being treated for another condition. While HACs can cause significant patient harm and substantial financial burden to the US health system, many HACs are preventable.

Acquired conditions research has generally focused on *hospital-*acquired conditions data, since these providers were the early adopters of quality and patient safety initiatives and have more agencies gathering data on outcomes. Not every healthcare provider type experiences all of the HACs outlined in this section; however post-acute and ambulatory care settings will experience some incidents and conditions listed below. For example, patients in the post-acute and ambulatory care settings experience adverse drug events, falls, pressure ulcers, and CAUTI. Ambulatory Surgery Center (ASC) quality metrics include patient burns; falls; wrong site, side, patient, procedure, and implant; and all-cause hospital transfer/admission.

As outlined below, HAC prevention can yield substantial cost savings, markedly improve patient outcomes, and save lives—all essential elements of the value-based care movement. The following list shows the average cost per event for several high-occurring HACs.

Adverse Drug Events (ADEs)
Estimated cost per event: $1,000–$9,000[182]

Improper medication reconciliation or medication discrepancies account for roughly one of every three adverse events in healthcare facilities, affect nearly two million patients each year, and prolong a patient's stay by 1.7 to 4.6 days.[183]

Catheter-Associated Urinary Tract Infections (CAUTIs)
Estimated cost per event: $5,000–$30,000[184]

CAUTIs are the most commonly reported HAC. More than 560,000 patients develop CAUTIs each year, and rates are on the rise. CAUTIs are known to extend patient stays, increase costs, and contribute to patient morbidity and mortality.[185]

Central Line-Associated Bloodstream Infections (CLABSIs)
Estimated cost per event: $18,000–$95,000[186]

CLABSIs are associated with significant increases in patient morbidity, mortality, and costs—it is estimated that as many as 28,000 patients die from CLABSIs annually in US intensive care units.[187]

Clostridium Difficile (C. diff) Infections (CDIs)
Estimated cost per event: $4,000–$32,000[188]

182 "Joint Commission Outlines 11 Tenets of a Safety Culture," Risk Management News.
183 "National Action Plan for ADE Prevention," US Department of Health and Human Services, accessed September 24, 2019, https://health.gov/hcq/ade.asp.
184 "Joint Commission Outlines 11 Tenets of a Safety Culture," Risk Management News.
185 "ANA CAUTI Prevention Tool," American Nurses Association, accessed August 23, 2022, https://www.nursingworld.org/practice-policy/work-environment/health-safety/infection-prevention/ana-cauti-prevention-tool/.
186 "Joint Commission Outlines 11 Tenets of a Safety Culture," Risk Management News.
187 "Central Line-Associated Bloodstream Infections (CLABSI), Agency for Healthcare Research and Quality, accessed July 25, 2018, https://www.ahrq.gov/topics/central-line-associated-bloodstream-infections-clabsi.html.
188 "Joint Commission Outlines 11 Tenets of a Safety Culture," Risk Management News.

C. diff—a bacterium that causes diarrhea and colitis—is estimated to cause nearly half a million illnesses in the United States each year. Roughly 20 percent of patients who get C. diff will get it again, and nearly 10 percent of patients over age sixty-five with healthcare-associated C. diff infection will die within a month of diagnosis.[189] The cost of this is staggering—the infection causes 2.4 million inpatient hospital days per year and adds $1.5 billion to annual healthcare costs.[190]

Falls

Estimated cost per event: $3,000–$15,000[191]

Each year, 700,000 to 1,000,000 people in the United States fall in healthcare facilities,[192] and roughly 25 percent of them will suffer fall-related injuries, resulting in increased healthcare utilization, longer patient stays, higher costs, and greater liability. Patients who have serious injuries related to falls while in healthcare facilities average 6 to 12 days of additional patient stay time than comparable patients who did not fall.[193]

189 "What Is C. Diff?," Centers for Disease Control and Prevention, updated June 27, 2022, https://www.cdc.gov/cdiff/what-is.html#anchor_1540390280946.

190 "Reducing Clostridium Difficile Infections," Joint Commission Center for Transforming Healthcare, accessed August 23, 2022, https://www.centerfortransforminghealthcare.org/improvement-topics/reducing-c-diff-infections

191 "Joint Commission Outlines 11 Tenets of a Safety Culture," Risk Management News.

192 "Preventing Falls in Hospitals," Agency for Healthcare Research and Quality, accessed August 23, 2022, https://www.ahrq.gov/professionals/systems/hospital/fallpxtoolkit/index.html.

193 E. L. D. Bouldin et al., "Falls among Adult Patients Hospitalized in the United States: Prevalence and Trends," Journal of Patient Safety 9, no. 1 (March 2013): 13–17, https://www.ncbi.nlm.nih.gov/pmc/articles/PMC3572247/.

Obstetric Adverse Events (OBAEs)

Estimated cost per event: Up to $1,000[194]

Serious obstetrical adverse events—which include harm to either the mother or the infant—occur in approximately 9 percent of all US births.[195]

Pressure Ulcers

Estimated cost per event: $9,000–$21,000[196]

Each year more than 2.5 million patients in US acute-care facilities suffer from pressure ulcers/injuries. These healthcare-acquired pressure ulcers/injuries cause roughly 60,000 patients to die from their complications each year.[197]

Surgical Site Infections (SSIs)

Estimated cost per event: $12,000–$42,000[198]

SSIs are the second most common type of healthcare-acquired infections, accounting for 22 percent of all healthcare-acquired infections and 8 percent of deaths associated with healthcare-acquired infections.[199] SSIs cost the US healthcare system $3.5 to $10 billion annually.[200]

194 "Joint Commission Outlines 11 Tenets of a Safety Culture," Risk Management News.

195 "Safety Program for Perinatal Care," RTI International, accessed November 17, 2016, https://www.rti. org/impact/safety-program-perinatal-care.

196 "Joint Commission Outlines 11 Tenets of a Safety Culture," Risk Management News.

197 "Hospital Acquired Pressure Ulcers/Injuries (HAPU/I) Prevention," Joint Commission Center for Transforming Healthcare, updated October 7, 2020, https://www.centerfortransforminghealthcare.org/ en/improvement-topics/hospital-acquired-pressure-ulcers-prevention.

198 "Joint Commission Outlines 11 Tenets of a Safety Culture," Risk Management News.

199 "Surgical Site Infections," Joint Commission Center for Transforming Healthcare, accessed August 23, 2022, https://www.centerfortransforminghealthcare.org/improvement-topics/surgical-site-infections.

200 "Financial Impact of Surgical Site Infections," Eloquest Marketing, accessed July 11, 2018, https:// www.eloquesthealthcare.com/2018/07/11/financial-impact-of-surgical-site-infections-ssis/.

Ventilator-Associated Pneumonia (VAP)
Estimated cost per event: $19,000–$80,000[201]

VAP is a complication that occurs in as many as 28 percent of patients who receive mechanical ventilation and is the leading cause of death from healthcare-acquired infection. VAP increases patient stay duration by an average of 7 days.[202]

Venous Thromboembolism (VTE)
Estimated cost per event: $11,000–$32,000[203]

It is estimated that up to 900,000 VTEs occur each year in the United States, resulting in approximately 100,000 patient deaths. VTE mortality alone costs the United States $8 to $10 billion in direct medical costs each year, not including the costs of associated complications.[204]

Noting the opportunity for improved HAC prevention, CMS in 2014 set a goal of reducing HACs by 20 percent by 2019. They estimated that this 20 percent reduction would result in 1.8 million fewer patients with HACs, 53,000 fewer deaths, and $19.1 billion in hospital cost savings in those five years alone.[205] In a 2017 report, AHRQ estimates showed that national efforts to reduce HACs helped

201 "Joint Commission Outlines 11 Tenets of a Safety Culture," Risk Management News.
202 Jean-Francois Timsit et al., "Update on Ventilator-Assisted Pneumonia," F1000 Research 6 (November 29, 2017), https://www.ncbi.nlm.nih.gov/pmc/articles/PMC5710313/.
203 "Joint Commission Outlines 11 Tenets of a Safety Culture," Risk Management News.
204 "Venous Thromboembolism (VTE) Prevention," Joint Commission Center for Transforming Healthcare, accessed August 23, 2022, https://www.centerfortransforminghealthcare.org/improvement-topics/venous-thromboembolism-prevention.
205 Agency for Healthcare Research and Quality (2019). Retrieved August 24, 2022, from chrome-extension://efaidnbmnnnibpcajpcglclefindmkaj/https://www.ahrq.gov/sites/default/files/wysiwyg/professionals/quality-patient-safety/pfp/hacreport-2019.pdf.

prevent 20,500 deaths and save the US healthcare system $7.7 billion between 2014 and 2017.[206]

Declines in Hospital-Acquired Conditions

Clostridioides difficile Infections **-37%**

Adverse Drug Effects **-28%**

Venous Thromboembolisms **-17%**

Ventilator-Associated Pneumonias **-13%**

All Other HACs **-12%**

CLABSI* **-6%**

CAUTI** **-5%**

Falls **-5%**

There is still more to be accomplished when it comes to delivering improved outcomes and safer care, including ensuring that patients and staff have more of a voice in sharing observations to prevent

206 "AHRQ Analysis Finds Hospital-Acquired Conditions Declined by Nearly 1 Million from 2014–2017," Agency for Healthcare Research and Quality, updated January 29, 2019, https://www.ahrq.gov/news/newsroom/press-releases/hac-rates-declined.html.

* Central Line-Associated Blood Stream Infections

** Catheter-Associated Urinary Tract Infections

patient safety events from occurring and ensuring that providers focus on proactive data collection for the sake of measurable improvements. CMS and private health insurance companies will continue to link payments to patient outcomes for the foreseeable future, and the public will continue to expect greater transparency in the reporting of patient safety and quality of care to guide their decisions about where to seek treatment. Establishing and maintaining effective patient safety and quality programs as part of delivering care value is an effort that can both improve patient outcomes and contribute to healthcare organizations' financial stability.

CHAPTER 9

Conclusion

Implementing actions to prevent patient and employee harm has the greatest potential effect on the quality and value of care delivered in our healthcare system.

M any of us in healthcare entered the profession to help, heal, and serve. At our cores, we are driven by compassion, empathy, and a desire to help people live their best lives. We know now that most medical errors are a result of flawed systems, not reckless practitioners. We also know that systems can learn from errors and improve, but only when those systems encourage reporting, transparently acknowledge their mistakes, and are held accountable for those errors.[207] Therefore, we must remain focused on creating organizational cultures that are centered around reporting as well as learning and using systems thinking to identify and resolve issues and to prevent harm from occurring.

Today, we also have a new breed of leaders emerging from within our healthcare organizations who are redefining patient and employee

---

207   "IHI and LLI Statement about the Risks to Patient Safety When Medical Errors Are Criminalized," Institute for Healthcare Review, updated March 20, 2022, http://www.ihi.org/about/news/documents/ IHI,%20LLI%20Statement_FINAL.pdf.

safety and reporting. These leaders are transforming their organizations into open, highly reliable safety cultures in which the reporting of near misses, unsafe conditions, and incidents presents opportunities to prevent harm from occurring or recurring. These leaders understand that strengthening prevention practices is at the center of the next transformation in patient safety and healthcare quality.

> The shift toward prevention requires that we pay as much attention to unsafe conditions and near misses as to more serious safety incidents.

The next decade in healthcare safety will have as its focus prioritizing the many voices engaged in the care experience: the voices of patients, their caregivers, and all healthcare workers. Only when we voice our observations and concerns in our work environments, when we listen to what others have to say about their experiences, and when we honor the findings that result from careful and thorough analysis can we address safety issues in the most effective way possible. When reporting is encouraged, errors are acknowledged, and accountability is more equitably distributed, we are able to learn from and improve the systems and processes that govern our work. It has been my claim throughout this book that the shift toward prevention in any patient safety initiative requires a robust reporting practice in order to provide a platform to those involved in the care process.

The shift toward prevention requires that we pay as much attention to unsafe conditions and near misses as to more serious safety incidents. The great value of reporting near misses and unsafe conditions is that they provide organizations with a fuller picture of what can be done to improve patient and employee safety, and they encourage more reporting of potential areas of risk before they become full-fledged incidents.

Establishing and maintaining a just culture of care requires a clear-eyed and courageous look at the imperfect and uncomfortable parts of our environments of care; this requires a commitment to listening, learning, and adjusting our practices intentionally and incrementally. The very concept of just culture is related to systems thinking, which emphasizes that patient safety incidents are generally the products of faulty systems and organizational cultures, rather than solely brought about by the person or persons directly involved. Broad staff input is one of the most valuable tools in healthcare. Our frontline caregivers, in particular, see it all. The more proactive they become about sharing observations, the safer our patients—and employees—will be. For this reason, driving active staff engagement has become a major strategy for increasing value and combating employee burnout and turnover.

As points of care continue to increase in number, and given that training levels vary, it is essential for healthcare leaders to establish a framework that sets caregivers up for success at every level and in every kind of organization. Right now, especially across the millions of post-acute, ambulatory, and social service centers, many care providers have yet to access supportive structures and technology tools that would improve their environments of care. As leaders in this arena, we must look at the wide range of healthcare facilities and ask ourselves: Do they have access to the resources needed to deliver safe, high-quality care?

The answer is, "Not yet." Most of the over 2.5 million points of care in the United States currently depend on patient safety and quality programs created in house or on paper, requiring manual entry of information and lacking data analytics tools to identify trends. Modernization may seem labored at first, but its longer-term results—including early intervention, prevention, overall reduction in serious safety events, and the saving of lives—are ultimately the drivers of innovation.

Modernizing safety and quality systems across all healthcare organizations is the next leap forward on the path to delivering the highest quality care in the safest possible environment. It's only when we choose to access this extraordinary opportunity to give care providers, patients, and patient families voices that we make strides toward the corresponding goals of better care, lower costs, safer employees, and safer patients.

Acknowledgments

I n the middle of a global pandemic that halted most businesses and sped up the need for technology to protect employees and patient safety, we reimagined our health tech company. The opportunity was a challenge, for sure—but one we, as a company, were ready to take on. On a personal level, this transition prompted a much broader question: how do I share with others all that I have learned through decades in healthcare to help them make an impact quickly? What you hold in your hands is my humble attempt at sharing this information so that you may make an impact way sooner than I ever did.

Like so many things in life, this book evolved with inspiration and help from others. Some of the greatest gifts I've received were unexpected. For instance, in 2010 a colleague asked if I would hire a recent master's degree graduate named Jessie Smith. Jessie's husband had one year remaining in law school, and she was looking for experience in healthcare administration until he graduated. At the time, I was spinning up my first healthcare company, and knowing I could use some help, I hired her. Not only has Jessie been vital in building Performance Health Partners; her steadiness, support, and guidance remain unmatched.

I want to thank the incredibly smart and talented Performance Health Partners team, especially Brandon Bergeron, all of whom wake up every morning thinking about how they are going to make a positive impact on others, be it a customer, their team members, or the software to enrich user experience. Together, they make it happen: Barbara Marhafer, Connie Christy, Mike Melito, Joe Cashia, David Callecod, Perla Soto, Ellie Songer, Mimsie Ladner, Savannah Montoya, Torey Hickman, Wendy Palmer, and many more. You are stars in the constellation that is PHP.

I would like to acknowledge the many others who, throughout my life, have helped me along my journey and who so often have shown me the way. There are far too many to list. Thank you.

I am especially thankful for the following individuals:

Mimsie Ladner, Courtney Pellegrini, and Doug Miller for research, graphics, and for providing creative sparks throughout this process.

Jen Pearl, this book began on a snowshoe trail in the Rockies with ideas entered into an iPhone. Thank you for introducing me to solitude and Utah snow.

My book coach and editor, Jen Holt, who has helped authors like me realize their full potential for many years. Thank you for choosing me to dedicate your time and talent. I could not have asked for a more engaged, diligent, and patient guide throughout this process of writing and editing. Our collaboration has allowed my story to come to life.

Trudi Stafford, whose contribution to this book and to the field of nursing, patient safety, and quality care is so vast that it cannot be measured. You are an inspiration to all of us.

Leslie Jacobs, my professional mentor and now friend, "saw" me and my potential long before others. Our "come to Leslie" conversations have pushed me to go beyond what I realized my potential was at any given moment.

PK Sheerle, RN, who gave me the best two sentences of business advice. Your words opened pathways in my mind that placed me on the professional trajectory I am on today.

Lindsay Wells. We began this professional journey together over 12 years ago, and I am grateful to grow alongside you.

The women leaders who guide me possess a rare combination of vision, perseverance, and passion; Kacie Kelly, Aparna Falgoust, Gretchen Cormier, Rebekah Gee, Liz Privitera, Lacy Culpepper, Marsha Miller, Amy Vaughan, Rebecca Hutchings, and Madelyn Meyn.

Amy Redmond, my sister, with whom I share a special bond. You are the keeper of memories and champion of friendships.

• • •

Last but never least, my daughters, Cecilia, Camille, and Marie, and my husband, Danny, who endured the writing and reading of the many, many edits to this book and, each time, offered encouragement and insight. Being a child of or married to an entrepreneur and CEO requires patience for late nights and missed events. Through it all, my family has supported my endeavors, and for this, I am grateful. Coming home to you is always the best part of each day.

About the Author

Heidi Raines is a healthcare executive and entrepreneur working at the intersection of patient and employee safety, systems innovation, and technology. She has dedicated her career to designing solutions to ensure that healthcare organizations have access to the knowledge and technology needed to deliver safe, equitable, and quality care.

Raines is the founder and CEO of Performance Health Partners, the leading software for patient and employee safety. She holds a Preceptor Faculty position at Tulane University's Master of Health Administration program and serves as Board President of the American College of Healthcare Executives Women's Healthcare Executive Network. Raines has received awards for innovation and executive leadership and was named one of the Top 100 Influential Entrepreneurs in Technology.

CPSIA information can be obtained
at www.ICGtesting.com
Printed in the USA
BVHW090918030123
655384BV00017B/223